The
Book of ECK Parables

Also by Harold Klemp

Ask the Master, Book 1
The Book of ECK Parables, Volume 1
The Book of ECK Parables, Volume 2
The Book of ECK Parables, Volume 3
Child in the Wilderness
The Living Word
Soul Travelers of the Far Country
The Spiritual Exercises of ECK
The Temple of ECK
The Wind of Change

The Mahanta Transcripts Series

Journey of Soul, Book 1
How to Find God, Book 2
The Secret Teachings, Book 3
The Golden Heart, Book 4
Cloak of Consciousness, Book 5
Unlocking the Puzzle Box, Book 6
The Eternal Dreamer, Book 7
The Dream Master, Book 8
We Come as Eagles, Book 9

MAHANTA

This book has been authored by and published under the supervision of the Living ECK Master, Sri Harold Klemp. It is the Word of ECK.

The
Book of
ECK Parables

Harold Klemp
Volume 4

ECKANKAR
Minneapolis, MN

Compiled by Mary Carroll Moore
Edited by Joan Klemp
Anthony Moore

Text illustrations by Tom Elliott
Cover photo by Bree Renz

Library of Congress Cataloging-in-Publication Data
(Revised for vol. 4)
Klemp, Harold.
    The book of ECK parables.
    1. Eckankar. 2. Parables. I. Title
BP605.E3K55 1986   299'.93   86-82644
ISBN 1-57043-017-9

Contents

Chapter Five: FAMILY AND RELATIONSHIPS

Chapter Six: DIVINE PROTECTION

Chapter Seven: SPIRITUAL TESTS AND SPIRITUAL GROWTH

Chapter Eight: SPIRITUAL EXERCISES
OF ECK

Chapter Nine: HEALTH AND HEALING

Chapter Ten: THE LIGHT AND SOUND

Chapter Eleven: BECOMING A CO-WORKER WITH GOD

Chapter Twelve: TIPS FOR MASTERSHIP

Introduction

You may wonder what a book full of stories has to do with the long journey to God. Aren't stories too simple, too everyday to illustrate lofty spiritual truths? After all, they're about people like you and me, people who have jobs and families, problems and joys.

But stories stick where philosophy doesn't. If you're like most people, you read a profound truth one minute but forget it the next. A story will linger in the heart and mind. Like a spiritual seed it will sprout at the perfect instant to give aid when you are facing a puzzling task or obstacle.

Like the story about the Swedish couple visiting America for the first time. They learn something about love when the wife unexpectedly meets a rock musician and his dog in the hotel elevator. Or the one about the Chinese fortune cookie that taught a businessman a lesson in respect. Or the old man who helped a young man learn about hard work, dreams, and turning dust to gold.

The Holy Spirit is always working on your behalf to make you a better, more loving human being. All that prevents this is a lack of focus on God. This book will help increase and sharpen that focus and give you a toolbox of assistance for years to come.

A spiritual student of ECK always receives instruction at least three different times in three different ways, especially if it is an important spiritual insight.

Chapter One

ECK Dream Teachings

1. The Three Trucks

One night in the dream state an ECK initiate found herself with the Inner Master, her spiritual guide. The Master was showing her a newspaper photo of a truck.

As she was looking at the photo, she remembered something unusual that had happened earlier. Three different times during the past month she had seen big trucks driving off the road. Each time the truck would suddenly drive off the road, make a U-turn, and get back on the road. The drivers hadn't seemed to pay much attention to the near accidents. The woman had thought it was strange at the time, but she didn't pay much attention to it until this dream came along.

When she woke up she thought a lot about the dream and the three trucks. "What do these three trucks mean?" she asked the Inner Master, who replied, "I think that's something you have to look at for yourself."

The image that struck her most was the truck going off the road. Why had the drivers been so careless? In a flash, she realized her dream and the three outer incidents were trying to tell her something: In her daily life she wasn't too careful either. She drifted here and there; she was often off course. When she planned carefully how to do one thing or another, she didn't go off on side roads and end up in a ditch.

The Mahanta, the Inner Master, was saying, "It would be a little easier on you if you made a plan and went for it, if you drove straight ahead and didn't wander off the road."

This was an example of an ECK principle: the chela, a spiritual student of ECK, always receives instruction at least three different times in three different ways, especially if it is an important spiritual insight. This is why I often recommend that the initiates keep dream journals. You have to have enough awareness to notice when the insights come.

2. The Riches of ECK

A woman had a dream where she was walking her dog down a street. Suddenly they came upon a very old suitcase. It was a large suitcase, but nobody seemed to own it. So the woman decided to take it home.

She bent to pick it up, juggling the dog's leash in one hand and the suitcase in the other. Just then a man walked up. "May I help?" he asked. She looked at him and realized it was Paul Twitchell, the modern-day founder of ECKANKAR.

"I'll help you carry it home," he said. "Thank you very much," she said. So he carried the suitcase toward her house.

When they got very close, Paul Twitchell told the woman, "This is as far as I go. You'll have to carry the suitcase the rest of the way yourself." Then he disappeared.

The woman got the suitcase home and opened it. It was full of money. "I can finally do all the things for other people that I've wanted to do," she said.

Very quietly she began giving this money to people. They didn't know where the money came from because she didn't need recognition for the gifts she gave.

When the woman awoke from the dream, she wondered what it meant. Then she realized the suitcase symbolized the riches of ECK, the Holy Spirit. Although she doesn't have much money in her life, she does have the true riches of ECK. She has the love of the Holy Spirit. No matter where she goes, she is able to give of this love to others.

Whenever I see people moving toward the polarity of power, I foresee all the problems they're going to cause—first for others and finally for themselves. But when I see an individual going along the path of love, such as this woman, I see a bright future for the person.

3. Operating Room

A Nigerian doctor did his spiritual exercises regularly and often met with the Dream Master, his inner spiritual guide, at night. One night the Dream Master took him to an operating room. In front of him were an array of surgeon's tools. He knew immediately what he had to do.

In the dream, the doctor began working on his patient, and as he operated, he found that the patient had a hernia. At first he thought he had solved the problem, but a voice in the dream said, "Look a little farther." So he looked farther and saw, in addition to the hernia, there was an obstruction off to the side. He went through the entire operation in the dream, step by step and in full awareness.

Soon after he woke up the next morning, the doctor got a call from his brother who was also a physician. The brother had a patient who had certain symptoms that were confusing. As his brother described this man and his illness, the ECKist recognized the patient. It was the same person he had operated on in the dream the night before. "Take this patient straight to the hospital," he instructed his brother. "Set up the operating room. I'll be right there."

The ECKist doctor performed the operation exactly as he had the night before in his dream. He saw a hernia, but because the Dream Master had tipped him off in his dream to look beyond the hernia for an obstruction, he did. Much to his surprise he found one. So he took care of it.

In discussing the case with his brother later, the ECKist doctor realized that the patient might have died if he hadn't found and removed this obstruction. The man's life was saved because of the dream.

For people who do the spiritual exercises and keep their hearts open, such experiences happen very often. Then there are other people who don't bother with the spiritual exercises; they don't have the personal discipline. They are the ones who complain that ECK doesn't work for them. What is this saying about the person? He's not putting his heart into his search for God.

4. Meeting ECK Masters

A man had been visited by different spiritual travelers since he was a baby. It began one night when he was lying in his crib. He was about two or three years old, and he remembers looking out the window at some stars.

Then he noticed one star that began to move sideways, first left, then right.

Suddenly the star came zooming toward earth, right through the boy's bedroom window. It became two stars, a blue one and a white one. An instant later two spiritual travelers stood there in the bedroom. They glowed with light and goodness. They were ECK Masters who work on the inner planes to teach Soul.

One of the spiritual travelers looked at the child. "Don't be afraid," he said. "We came to you because of your love."

The boy climbed out of his crib and went to wake his parents. As he was walking toward their bed, he heard one of the spiritual travelers say, "He's not ready yet." Then they were gone.

The next time this young person ran into an ECK Master was when he was living in Indiana as a college student. He was on his way to the library when a very tall beggar approached him. The beggar with very clear eyes looked at the young man and said, "Excuse me, could I borrow two dollars?"

5. Isle of Bliss

A dreamer awoke in a dream and saw three children coming toward her down a maze of streets. As the children approached her, one of them asked, "Do you know where our father is?"

Since the dreamer had been this route before, she said, "Sure." And she gave them directions to find their father.

Two of the children ran off very quickly because that was all the information they needed. But the third child seemed to be having difficulties. He was a little slower in walking. So the dreamer went with him through the streets.

They had a pleasant conversation, talking about one thing or another, until they came to a window in a wall. The window was decorated with lights and little teddy bears.

The dreamer turned to the little boy. "Here's the window," she said, "but I don't know how you're going to get through it," thinking about the difficulty he had walking. "Oh, I know how," said the child. "And when I get through it, I will get in a boat and row to the island. My father will be waiting there."

When the dreamer awoke, she realized this had been a highly significant dream. The three children were Souls saying, "Do you know where we can find the Inner Master, our spiritual guide?" The third child had karmic problems which made it difficult for him to progress on the spiritual path.

The island in the ECKist's dream where the little boy would meet his father symbolized the Isle of Bliss, which all Souls seek.

The dreamer was grateful for the dream. It reassured her that no matter how inadequate she sometimes felt about her knowledge of ECK, she had something to give to other people. She could act as a guide on the inner planes, working with the Holy Spirit to show people how to make the spiritual connection with the Mahanta, their spiritual guide.

6. Trying to Forget

A young girl had had a very difficult child-hood. When she was only eleven, her brother died unexpectedly. This left her feeling very sad. At the same time she contracted tuberculosis and required a lung operation.

During her recuperation, she began having dreams. In the dreams, she was instructed several times, "Find ECK. Find ECKANKAR." When she got out of the hospital, she looked every-where—in dictionaries, in encyclopedias—trying to find these strange words *ECK* and *ECKANKAR*. But she found nothing.

About a year later, her grandparents were in a serious car accident. At about 1:00 a.m. she had a vivid dream where a man in a blue shirt and blue slacks came to her grandmother and took her to the other side.

The young girl woke up and went downstairs to tell her father. "I just had a dream," she said. "A man in blue took my grandmother across to the other side." Living in a remote area, the family had no telephone. It wasn't until the next day that an aunt drove to the house and brought the news: the grandmother had died the previous night around 1:00 a.m.

Having seen this event put a terrible strain on the girl. She knew where her father kept some bourbon and other alcoholic drinks high up in a cabinet. So one day she started drinking. Like a little bird fallen out of a nest before it could fly, she had seen something before she was able to handle it.

For the next fourteen years, the girl lived pretty much in a drunken stupor, trying to forget what she had seen. The alcohol made her forget. She found that the more she drank, the less she remembered about the inner experiences.

Finally the drinking got too much for her, and she gave it up. As soon as she did, she met a man with the happiest face she had ever seen. After they had gotten better acquainted, he began talking to her about his religion.

When he said the word *ECKANKAR*, she almost ended the relationship. All the memories of her grandmother's death and her experience with the dream prophecy came flooding back.

But the woman was stronger now. This man was still the happiest person she'd ever met. A little time later they were married and, as far as I know, are still living together happily.

Sometimes a dream comes too soon. The dream says, "There's a bigger, brighter world waiting for you. When the time is right, you'll be ready to enter this world and enjoy a fuller life than you can ever imagine."

It's a very fearful time when people come to the point of outgrowing their state of consciousness. If by chance they should have an experience in the dream worlds before they are spiritually grown up, they're going to misread it.

But Soul never forgets the experience. It sticks in the mind of the individual until he or she is ready to fly freely and enter a whole new world.

hat, an old pipe hanging out of his mouth, and ragged clothes.

I waved to him. "Seen a lot of those wagons going by lately?" I asked, subtly trying to find out what year it was. "Well, folks didn't use them as much before the war," the man replied. "He's probably talking about the Civil War," I told the chela. "It's been about fifteen years that we've seen a lot of those, since right after the war," the man added. I mentally added fifteen to 1865.

"This must be about 1880," I said to the initiate beside me. You can't just go up to someone and ask, "What year is this? It somehow slipped my mind." The old man had a flintlock by him, and he probably wouldn't feel especially comfortable if we asked such a thing.

The chela and I went a little farther, and we came to some underground caverns. I showed him where there was an underground city, then we went through a walkway back to the Astral Plane. From there he was able to wake up back in the physical body.

Soul always works in the present moment. It's a little difficult to explain, but the past and future are all contained in the present. We think of the past as a dead image, but it's actually still occurring in memory. When you get there, it looks as real as anything you could ever know. The future is the same. Soul stands on a promontory in the present moment, and It can look at both the past and the future.

In the dream, we had moved to the Causal Plane, the place of memory. We had gone through the energy field. We saw the Conestoga wagons and the pioneers whipping their oxen. The wagons were going down a rutted road that was probably the Oregon Trail.

I'm always kind of disappointed when I get a letter from a person like this chela who writes, "I can't remember my dreams. Is there something you can do?" I want to write back to him and just say, "1880."

8. Journal Notes

A young woman from Melbourne, Australia, sat next to me on a plane. During the flight she reached into her luggage and pulled out a journal. She began making notes.

As she kept writing and writing, I wondered what such a young person could have to write about. You have to have some kind of experience before you would even bother to pick up a pen and start filling pages of a notebook.

I didn't talk with her because she was so busy. She wrote for several hours. When the plane was coming into Sydney, I whispered to my wife, "I've got to ask her what she's writing—but mostly, I've got to ask her why. If I don't, I'll wonder about it for the rest of my life."

She told me she was a college student. She had been traveling in North America for four months during the summer. She said she had had a lot of experiences and the four months had passed very quickly. Her travels had taken her throughout the United States, Canada, and Mexico. She had had a good trip, but now it was time to come home.

She said, "I want to write down my experiences while they are fresh. Maybe five, ten, or fifteen years from now I'll read them again and remember the trip."

She realized that very few points in the journal were of great significance to her now. "But at some time in the future, I'll be able to look back at these notes and see myself as a person who had had great experiences," she told me. I thought this was very insightful. It's one reason I ask the initiates in ECK to keep a dream journal.

ECKists ask me, "Why should I write my dreams down? When I have dreams, they're clear to me." They don't realize that a few might turn out to predict the future or give some insight into the individual's life. Sometimes this comes clear only when you read them months or years later.

9. Flying about Town

A Second Initiate lived in an apartment. She had learned to Soul Travel in her dreams but often wondered why she never seemed to travel any farther than her apartment building.

Each time she fell asleep and woke up in the Soul body, she was able to see her Physical body lying on the bed. She would generally walk through her front door and out into the hallway of her building. And then she'd wait awhile.

Pretty soon, the Inner Master would come around the corner. "Where do you want to go?" he'd ask the woman. And she'd answer, "I want to go to a Golden Wisdom Temple." But the only place she went was her apartment building.

One night she asked the Inner Master why she never seemed to go anywhere else in her dreams. "Please show me what I need to do," she said.

"How did you learn to Soul Travel?" he asked. So she began thinking about the first time she had found herself out of the body.

She had walked into the kitchen, into the bedroom, and looked around a little. "Hey, this is great," she had said. Each step of the way she'd thought of what to do next. It took her awhile in the dream state to think of chanting Wah Z, the spiritual name of the Inner Master, but she finally did. This took her to another level. Then she felt she ought to be doing something else, but it took another bit of time for her to think of sitting on the couch and doing a spiritual exercise.

The spiritual exercise took her out of her apartment into the hallway where she met the Inner Master. This had been the last experiment she tried.

Finally she understood why the Master didn't come up to her and just say, "OK, we'll go off to a Wisdom Temple. I'll do everything for you; you don't have to do anything." The Dream Master was letting her use her own creativity.

Most often a person fails at Soul Travel or dream travel because inside the individual is the fear of death. As this ECKist began to experiment and have the experience of Soul Travel under her own terms, it began to diminish this fear.

10. Dream Payment

In a dream, a woman saw her husband opening the mail. In one envelope was a large check. She saw the amount and also saw her husband write her a check for part of the total. When she woke up, she thought this was a very nice dream.

That morning she was talking with her husband and her daughter in the kitchen. "You know," she said, "last night I had a dream where you got a check in the mail for around twenty-four hundred dollars. And you gave me six hundred dollars from the check."

Her husband looked at her and started laughing. He walked out of the room and came back with a check. "I got this in the mail yesterday," he said, holding up a check for $2440.

And because she had guessed right, he added, "Six hundred is for you."

Not all dreams work out well and turn a profit. But sometimes a dream can turn up a surprisingly nice side.

This is why I encourage people to study their dreams. The dream state is such an interesting place to meet people and visit different places. And as you live and move and have your being on the inner planes at night while the physical body sleeps, you can have fantastic and enjoyable experiences.

11. Lewis's Translation

Lewis was a twenty-five-year-old bachelor who lived in a town in West Africa. He had just gotten a very good job offer with an oil-drilling company. One of a hundred applicants for that position and the only one who did not have a degree in higher education, Lewis was put through a battery of tests for the specialized work on a very sophisticated computer.

One of the members of the interview team argued, "We should disqualify this candidate from the testing because he doesn't have a degree from a school of higher education." But another member of the team was more lenient. "Let's give Lewis a fair chance," he said. "He's here. He's had three months of training on another computer, and he's shown some expertise here. Let him take the test."

Each candidate was given fifteen minutes to work out a series of complex problems. Lewis got the highest marks of all the candidates. When he was announced as the person chosen for the job, one of the other candidates came up to him.

"Throughout this entire review, I have noticed how calm you are. You have such confidence, and I've been struck by your happy countenance." Lewis smiled and thanked her.

That evening Lewis visited an ECKist friend. "I have two things to tell you," Lewis said to his friend. "First, I have been accepted for a very good position with an oil company." He told his friend the story of the interview and the testing. "The reason I did so well on the computer," Lewis said, "is because the Mahanta has been teaching me on the inner planes how to run it. When it came time to take the test on the physical computer, it was very easy."

Then he said, "The second thing I have to tell you is this: I am going to translate (die) in about six weeks."

The ECK initiate just about fell over. Lewis was a young man at the beginning of a very promising and brilliant career. "How do you know?" asked the friend.

"I had a dream," explained Lewis. "I'm going to translate soon."

The ECKist said, "You must be mistaken about the meaning of your dream."

"No," Lewis said, "I went back to the Inner Master and asked for verification. The Master said that yes, indeed, the dream was true; in six weeks, I will translate."

Lewis explained how he had asked the Master, "Could the time be postponed for a little while?" He had some things to take care of before he went. "Of course it can," the Master said. And a postponement was arranged.

So Lewis began to get his outer affairs in order. For a week or two, he wore a very worried look on his face. He had become attached to the human body, to his life, and his friends. For a minute the teachings from his Christian past came creeping in.

But after a time Lewis returned to his usual cheerful confidence and good, loving nature. He visited the ECKist again one morning.

"The company has decided to send me to the United States for additional training within the next month," Lewis told his friend. The date of his translation and his travel to the U.S. would happen very close together.

During his last week Lewis asked his friend to go with him to a lawyer to make up a will. Then Lewis went back to his hometown and distributed gifts to his ECK friends. He told a few of them of his impending translation, he gave them gifts, and they had a very happy last supper together. And then he went to bed.

Very quietly during the night, Lewis translated.

Lewis's death was totally unexpected by most; he was a very healthy man as far as anyone else could see. But because of his dream with the Inner Master, he had had time to prepare, to give his love to other people, to finish his life here.

Translation is a fact of life, a very natural step into the other worlds. It's a continuation of life. Dreams can help us understand it better.

and understood what Yaubl Sacabi was saying.

Yaubl spoke to her in her dreams many times as a child. He always had to speak above the angry scolding of his father. Yaubl explained the spiritual wisdom of ECK to this little girl who also felt useless and unwanted. Many years later, as an adult, she found the ECK teachings.

On the inner planes, the ECK Masters, these great spiritual beings, come to help each person as that individual needs it at that very moment, regardless of age.

13. Guillotine Dream

A man from Canada had finished a hard day's work and was lying on the couch at home, watching TV. He was so tired that he dozed off. Sometime later he woke up. A movie about the French revolution was just coming to an end.

It was an old black-and-white film. As he watched, some of the nobility were being led to their deaths at the guillotine.

A few nobles went to their deaths very calmly, without blinking an eye. The man watching the movie thought they really lived up to their nobility. Others went kicking and screaming, cursing the guards.

Still sleepy, the man found himself wondering how he would have done in the same situation.

During sleep that night, the Dream Master came to him and showed him the same black-and-white movie about the French revolution. The Dream Master said, "In a second you will be in the movie." The man said, "I don't want to be in the movie."

The Dream Master said, "You've got to be in the movie. You will understand later." The next thing the dreamer knew, he was in the movie; two revolutionaries were dragging him up to the guillotine. He felt ashamed because he was kicking and screaming, cursing everyone. He was led up to the platform, his head was put into the guillotine, and he heard the blade whistling down.

Suddenly he was out of the body. It was effortless, and the Dream Master was beside him. The Dream Master told him, "Whenever you have a thought, it has life."

People don't realize that idle thoughts without the protection of Divine Spirit become little karmic things to resolve sometime later. You protect yourself by singing HU, a sacred name of God. You sing HU and say, "I don't really need that experience."

In ECK you can also work these things out in the dream state. You don't have to go through the wear and tear out here in the physical body.

Life doesn't necessarily become easier for someone who's in ECK. But the lessons that you do have will be those that are absolutely necessary for you, those that are not possible for you to get in any other way.

14. First Connection

A woman in Australia had been living in a house with her mate for four years. Then the relationship broke up, and the woman found herself living in a dingy little apartment.

She asked the landlord if she could do something to brighten up the place, so that it would be a quiet haven to come home to. The landlord said, "Sure," so she spent time painting and cleaning up.

Many of her belongings stayed in boxes for several months. One day she decided to unpack a box of books. There in the box was *The Flute of God* by Paul Twitchell. This was before she knew anything about ECKANKAR. She couldn't remember buying the book; she had never seen it before. But as she held the book in her hand, she saw that the yellow cover was exactly the same color as she had just painted her apartment.

She turned the book over and on the back cover she saw the photo of Paul Twitchell, the ECK Master whose spiritual name is Peddar Zaskq. And she recognized him as the person who had been coming to her in her dreams for nine months.

The first time she'd seen him, she'd been asleep in her room. Suddenly she felt the presence of someone. She opened her eyes and noticed a light in her bedroom. This light grew brighter and brighter until it filled the entire room. In the center of the light stood Paul Twitchell. He came to her and put his hands above her, not touching; she could feel the power and the love of God which took away all her fears.

Finally she asked him, "Who are you? What are you doing here?" He said, "Be quiet." He was telling her to just accept the love. This was during months of hard emotional times in her life, and he came back on a few more occasions.

As she looked at the book in her hand, she said, "This man who supposedly died in 1971 came and talked with me." She wondered so much about her dream experiences that she decided to write ECKANKAR. But she wasn't sure whether to mail the letter.

A few days before she decided to mail the letter, Paul Twitchell came to her again. He came out of the light and said, "You now have the Light and Sound of God," and then he left.

The outer teachings of ECK cannot tailor the spiritual clothing closely enough to fit each person individually, but they do provide a gateway. They are stepping-stones into the other worlds. It's in the other worlds that you get exactly the insights, wisdom, and source of love that you need at that particular moment in your life.

15. Good Friends

A woman and her mother were good friends. One day the woman came to visit her mother, but the mother was in a hurry. She had an appointment with the eye doctor, so the two women only had a few minutes to chat.

The mother had always been a person who was very afraid of death. She usually worried a lot about how things would turn out. But on this particular day she looked at her daughter and said, "I've learned something in all these years. Sometimes it's better not to know something, because then you don't worry about it." They were joking about her sixtieth birthday which would be in a few days.

Two hours later as the mother was coming home from the eye doctor, she was killed in a car accident. A message kept coming gently into the daughter's mind, "Your mother will teach you more through her death than she did in life." The daughter didn't quite know what this meant.

During the next two years she met with her mother in the dream state a number of times. Sometimes the dream experiences were so real, she knew she was actually there. Her mother was alive, well, and happy. But the daughter kept wondering, Where is this place I see my mother? Why am I so happy when I come back?

Around that time the daughter was enrolled

in some classes on religion. One day the teacher said, "Today we're going to have a guest speaker who's going to talk with us about ECKANKAR." As she listened, the daughter began to get certain insights into what happened to her mother.

Everyone finds ECK by a unique route. Sometimes parents and children are not close, but it's one of the most enjoyable things when there is a deep love between the family members. The love the mother had for her daughter played a part in the young woman's new understanding that Soul lives forever.

Soul picks Its own path to God in Its own time, in Its own way.

Contemplations . . .

When you have a nightmare, pursue the nightmare. Pursue the dream. Find out why it's happening. Don't become the pursued; become the hunter, the pursuer in your own dream worlds.

* * *

Dreams are another face of reality, just as this everyday life is a dream. For some people, dreams are so real they can't separate them from everyday life. Their inner and outer lives are woven into one whole unit of spiritual existence.

* * *

Some people say their dreams fade away so fast when they wake. Others remember dreams easily. It's a matter of consciousness. Like an early spring flower, some people unfold sooner than others. It's the individuality of Soul. Soul picks Its own path to God, at Its own time, in Its own way.

* * *

People ask, "Why should I keep a dream journal? When I do have dreams, they're clear to me." They don't realize that a few might turn out to predict the future or give some insight into the individual's life.

* * *

The dream state is such an interesting place to go. You can see different people and visit different places. And as you live, move, and have your being on the inner planes at night while the physical body sleeps, you can have fantastic and enjoyable experiences. But above all, they're highly educational.

When you're walking your own path to God,
you often recognize the message of truth that is given
to you. You take the kernel of truth, and you go on.

Chapter Two

Waking Dreams and the Golden-tongued Wisdom

16. Fortune Cookie

An ECKist went to lunch with a friend. During lunch the man told the ECKist a funny joke about a fat couple he had happened to see sitting next to him in another restaurant. The ECKist went away from the lunch meeting thinking that it was a really funny story. And he filed it away to pass on later.

That evening the ECKist was at a Chinese restaurant with a business associate. When they finished their meal, the waitress brought the check with two fortune cookies. Just as the ECKist started to break open his fortune cookie, a large couple came into the restaurant and were seated at the next booth. The couple reminded him of the people in the funny story he had heard earlier.

While the ECKist was breaking open his fortune cookie, he leaned over to his friend. "I heard the funniest story today," he whispered, and he began telling the story about the fat couple to his friend.

Pausing to give effect to the punch line, he happened to glance down at the message inside his fortune cookie: "When one speaks only good about others, there is no need to whisper," the slip of paper said.

This is an example of the Golden-tongued Wisdom. When the ECKist saw the fortune, he knew right away that the ECK, or Holy Spirit, was giving him a very direct message: Be advised, think again. If you're speaking good, why whisper?

His friend urged him, "Go on with the story; I want to hear it." But the ECKist said, "No, I'd rather not," and showed him the fortune. "I don't think I want to hear it now," laughed the man.

When you're walking your own path to God, you often recognize the message of truth that is given to you. You take the kernel of truth, and you go on. You may not understand the full impact of the message at that point, but likely as not, it'll come into your consciousness a couple of weeks later, and it will build upon some other experience where you forgot again.

17. The Australian Schoolteacher

A teacher in Australia had finished a particularly rough day with her students. She taught French to children ages seven or eight. Because it was hot they were unruly that day, and she couldn't do anything to maintain order in the classroom.

A citywide train strike was on that week. Instead of taking a ten-minute train ride home, after school let out that evening the teacher had to get on the bus and ride for several hours. The buses were very overcrowded because of the strike, and there was no air conditioning.

Sitting near the front of the bus, the woman mulled over what had happened during the day. Inwardly she seethed. How difficult the children had been! Her thoughts went round and round as she got angrier.

Suddenly the bus driver's radio crackled as a communication came through. Another driver was calling the command center. "The needle on my heat gauge is going up and up," he said. "What do I do?"

The command center radioed back: "Is it in the yellow or the red zone of the heat gauge?" Over the radio came the answer: "It's in the red." "Well, slow down," the voice said, "so the bus can cool off."

The ECK, or Holy Spirit, was sending a message to the teacher through the Golden-tongued Wisdom: "Hey, cool down, take it easy. The students were unruly because it was a hot day. And you're going to need more patience to get through the rest of it." She didn't get the message, though.

A little bit later, the bus arrived at a corner. The driver was driving pretty quickly, trying to make up time. But three students were standing out in the street, so the bus had to slow down as it swung around the corner. "Some people won't move even if you drive over their toes," the driver grumbled. He stopped the bus and gestured to the students, who stepped back onto the curb. Then the bus took off.

Again the ECK was telling her, "Give up your anger of the day. Back off. Let it go. Leave it in the classroom; don't carry it home with you." But she still couldn't hear it.

When the bus driver put on his right-turn signal and began to make a right turn, a car came up on the right side and tried to squeeze past. The driver of the bus and the driver of the car both stopped. The bus driver leaned out the window. "You've got to be joking," he said to the driver of the car. "Can't you see the signal?"

Finally the ECK teacher got the message. "You've got to be joking; can't you see the signals?" the ECK was saying to her.

This is a very simple example of the waking dream. This sort of experience goes on in your life every day. These things pop up to help you through your day, through your life. But you need the awareness to let you know when and how to listen.

18. Duck!

A friend called late one evening to talk. He said he'd been doing a lot of volunteer work for ECK, and some people had taken exception to it.

I was trying to explain to him that when you do work for ECK, the Holy Spirit, you sometimes have to keep a low profile. But he didn't quite understand what I was saying. He went on to describe the number of different ways people had misunderstood his motives as he was trying to serve God.

Just then right outside my open window came a loud, "Quack, quack, quack!" So I said into the phone, "Did you hear that?" He said, "No." "Duck," I said. He said, "What?"

"Duck," I repeated. "If you don't want people to attack you for serving ECK, duck. Keep a low profile."

Later in our conversation, it happened again. He was telling me other problems that had occurred, and right outside the window came, "Quack, quack, quack."

"Did you hear that?" I asked my wife. She went to the window, but the duck was gone.

Three times the duck came that evening during our telephone call. Three times I told this person, "Duck."

This is what we call the Golden-tongued

Wisdom. Often the Divine speaks to us in the humblest ways. I am supposed to be able to give all this great wisdom to somebody, and I try my best. But sometimes I don't quite have the right words. I didn't have the words to help this person around his problem.

Most people overlook the ways that the Holy Spirit speaks to us. It's not that the ways are too humble. It's that the people are too proud to listen. Divine Spirit speaks to us through Its creatures and through nature. It shows us how the Law of God can work if we have the spiritual understanding to see it.

19. The Rented Bicycle

A Higher Initiate in ECKANKAR had been concerned for a while about her lack of inner experience. She did her spiritual exercises every day, but the Sound and Light of God, which had been her constant inner companions for years, seemed to have disappeared.

One time she had a brief experience with the Light, but all she saw in front of her inner vision was a wall made up of enormous rocks. I must be facing a wall, she thought. But she didn't know what to do to get around it.

That summer the woman went to the ECK European Seminar in the Netherlands. Because they were staying in a hotel by the beach, she and two friends rented bicycles to travel to the downtown seminar site.

The first day the trio set out for the seminar on their bicycles. The woman's friends started jingling the little bells on their bikes. Her bell didn't work. Joking, she said to her friends, "I have no bell. I can't hear the Sound." Knowing her spiritual concerns at that time, her friends laughed at the coincidence.

The women were bicycling back to their hotel that evening when it began to get dark. "It would be really funny if your light didn't work," the two friends said to the Higher Initiate. They stopped at a restaurant for dinner and left the bicycles outside. After dinner, they started toward the hotel. The Higher Initiate's bicycle light wouldn't work. Then her seat came loose and almost fell off.

The woman was in a predicament. Bicycling along, she had no bell to warn pedestrians she was coming, no light to show her the way, and no solid support. She could barely hang on to the bicycle. "First thing in the morning, I'm going to take this bike in and exchange it for one that works," she said.

The next morning, the Higher Initiate got up early to go to the bike shop. As she was getting dressed, a friend came by. "I have to run a meeting," the friend said. "Could you please baby-sit my stepdaughter?" The Higher Initiate agreed, knowing she would have to ride the same bicycle to the seminar later that day. Somehow she managed.

Friends wanted to go see a fireworks display after the seminar, but the Higher Initiate had a nagging feeling she'd better get back to the hotel. So she thanked her friends and started off on her bicycle. Halfway there, she heard a flapping sound, then a clunk. Now the bicycle had a flat tire. This was the last straw.

Each time something had gone wrong with the woman's bike, her friends had gotten more and more concerned. Maybe they had taken each problem as a bad spiritual sign, she thought. They probably thought they should be riding with someone else.

Later the Higher Initiate noticed something different: Each time something broke on her bike, she got a stronger feeling of love and support from the Mahanta. Although the bike was breaking down, it was as if everything in her inner worlds was better taken care of.

That night she went into contemplation and chanted HU. She realized that the bicycle was a symbol for her mind. She had to drop the mind before she could go to the true spiritual planes. The bicycle breaking down was a way of saying that her mind was no longer capable of carrying her spiritually. A whole new chapter was opening up for her.

The bicycle experience was the Holy Spirit's way of telling her that she was now spiritually ready to go into the first of the true spiritual worlds, the Soul Plane.

20. Learning Grace

A woman sat down to do her contemplation one morning before she left for work. She asked the Inner Master, "What quality would help me grow the most spiritually?"

She expected the Inner Master to say, "The thing that will help you grow the most spiritually is love." Or, she thought, maybe he'll say it's joy.

The answer surprised her when it came through in contemplation very softly and quietly. "Grace," the Inner Master told her. She decided it must mean an attitude of thankfulness for the blessings of God. Living with this gratitude must be grace, she reasoned. Without thinking much more about it, she left for work.

Midway down the highway, a big truck cut her off, practically driving her off the road. Shaken, she pulled over to the shoulder to calm down. After she got over her shock, the woman was very angry. She could have been killed!

Then she remembered that she had just gotten the answer in contemplation: Grace. So she let go of her anger. She realized the truck driver probably had never even seen her.

Finally feeling steady enough to drive, she pulled back on the highway. She soon caught up with the slow-moving truck on a hill. As she was passing it, she saw on the side of the truck in great big letters: *Grace*.

Sometimes the Holy Spirit will make a connection between your inner worlds and the physical outer world, giving you confirmation of something in your heart. This is what we call a waking dream. The woman got the inner message from the Mahanta; then she got the outer message. She would learn to have grace, even under difficult circumstances. It was confirmation of what she had received in contemplation just a little while before.

21. Watch It!

One day my wife went to pick up my ECKANKAR mail. One of the staff helped her load it in the car.

The person helping her loaded the mail into the back of the car and closed the hatchback. With the extra weight the car began to roll a little, so my wife pulled up the emergency brake a tiny bit.

As she was leaving, she raised her arm to wave good-bye. Her watch fell off her wrist and slid down in her sleeve. She said to him, "That means watch it. The ECK is telling me to watch it." "What are you supposed to watch?" he asked. "I wonder," she mused.

So she drove home very carefully, checking the traffic and watching for people changing lanes unexpectedly. She got home OK, and I came out to meet her when I heard the car drive in.

"What's that burning smell?" I asked. "It smells like the brake is burning." My wife could smell it as well. We both looked inside the car and saw that the emergency brake was still on.

Since she doesn't usually use the emergency brake, she didn't think to release it when she left for home. The ECK, or Holy Spirit, working with a small detail of her life, was saying, "Hey, watch it. You left the brake on a little bit."

No harm was done. But this is an example of how the ECK will work in your life in the very smallest area, even when there isn't a major crisis. Some people like to learn about the past, but often the ECK is more helpful to us in the present when It shows us something to watch out for.

Contemplations . . .

Sometimes the Holy Spirit will make a connection between your inner worlds and the physical outer world, giving you confirmation of something in your heart. This is what we call a waking dream. It's an inner message from the Mahanta.

* * *

Soul in the lower worlds is often asleep. It's asleep with habits which prevent It from walking the direct path to God. We are trying to rise above this level in awareness. We are trying to reach a higher consciousness.

* * *

As you go further in ECK, you develop a greater awareness of what and who you are— where your circle begins and ends, and where the circles of other people begin and end. You begin to realize that when you do something, you are setting up effects out in the world, in the circles of other people.

* * *

When you're walking your own path to God, you recognize the message in the truth that is given to you. You take the kernel of truth, and you go on. You may not understand the full impact of the message at that point, but likely as not, it'll come into your consciousness a couple of weeks later, and it will build upon some other experience where you forgot again.

* * *

Most people overlook the ways that the Holy Spirit speaks to us. It's not that the ways are too humble. It's that the people are too proud to listen. Divine Spirit speaks to us through Its creatures and through nature. It shows us how the Law of God can work if we have the spiritual understanding to see it.

The dog was also Soul, responding to the divine love that comes down from the highest plane of God. The dog saw her need and understood.

Chapter Three

The Giving Heart

22. Listening to God

A certain woman was considered to be very strong by her friends. She was the person that others went to when they had trouble in their lives. But one morning she woke up feeling depressed, lonely, forgotten, and unloved. Seventeen years ago on this date her father had died, and she had kept her sorrow to herself all these years.

She felt terrible, but she went to work. Her boss was a very understanding person. "On a day like this, sometimes it's better just to forget work," he advised. "Go to some special place or talk with a special person." And the woman had someone in mind, a very close friend.

When she arrived at her friend's home, he was painting the garage. His dog Buck sat next to him. Buck had always been very unfriendly toward women and very protective of his owner. When he saw the woman approaching, Buck began to growl. The dog sat there growling at her as she watched her friend paint his garage.

This woman needed love, but she didn't know how to ask for it. She was too shy to say, I feel really down; I just need a hug. As her friend kept painting the garage, she felt worse and worse. Pretty soon he finished. But rather than come over and talk to her, he began cleaning his brushes. She sat on the steps watching him, feeling worse than ever. Buck had gone off somewhere, and she was glad. She didn't need him snarling at her.

Suddenly Buck crept up behind her. She stiffened and waited for him to start his usual growling. Instead, he licked her on the cheek, then sat down beside her and let her pet him.

The woman realized that the dog understood her need and had come to give her love because no one else would give it, mainly because she didn't know how to ask.

The dog was also Soul, responding to the divine love that comes down from the highest plane of God. The woman wasn't someone that others would expect needed any love; she was one of the "strong" people whom others asked for love. But the dog saw her need and understood.

23. The Swedish Couple and the Rock Musician

A man from Sweden told me a story about a certain Swedish couple. They were not very sophisticated travelers, but they wanted to visit New York City. When their friends learned of their plans, they warned the couple, "The crime is terrible. Be very careful And don't ride in the subway—all kinds of terrible muggings happen in the subway."

The couple finally arrived in New York, made it to their hotel safely, and even went on a few guided tours. But at the end of their stay, they had a few days left with nothing planned. They were afraid to go outside of their hotel room because of all the terrible things that could happen, according to their friends. But they were running short of refreshments.

So one morning the wife took her life in her hands and left the room to go to a convenience store down the block. As she stepped into the elevator, a huge man with a huge dog got on beside her. He was the leader of a rock band staying in the hotel, but the Swedish woman only saw the long hair, the dirty jeans, and the chains around his neck.

The woman was petrified. She stood in a corner of the elevator, shaking and saying over and over, "Oh, my God." All her friends' warnings came into her head. It seemed like her worst fears had walked right onto this elevator with her.

The dog, meanwhile, was curious about the woman. He came up to her and started to sniff her dress, as dogs do.

"Down," commanded the man to his dog. The dog lay down on the floor, and at the same time the Swedish woman flattened herself on the floor beside him.

At this, the musician began to laugh and laugh. He laughed until tears ran down his face. He laughed all the way out of the hotel and onto the street. The poor woman was so scared she crawled off the elevator on her hands and knees. Then she gathered her courage, stood up, and went to buy the refreshments. By the time she returned to the hotel room, she was too embarrassed to tell her husband what had happened.

That night the wife was afraid of running into the rock musician again, so she wanted to eat upstairs. But her husband was restless. He wanted to go to the hotel dining room. "Before we leave I want to see more of the people who live here," he said. They went down to the dining room, and there was the whole rock band, having dinner. As soon as the woman walked into the room, the whole band began to laugh uproariously. They laughed until tears ran down their faces and they had to leave.

In the days that followed, each time the Swedish couple came downstairs to eat in the hotel dining room, the rock band would be there.

The husband always wondered why they laughed so much whenever he and his wife entered the room.

Mercifully the day finally came when the couple packed their bags to return to Europe, back to their sane life. When they went to the front desk to pay their hotel bill, the desk clerk said, "Your bill's paid in full."

"How can this be?" asked the husband. They didn't know anybody in New York.

The clerk shrugged. "Here's a letter for the lady," he said, holding out an envelope. The Swedish woman opened it and began to read.

"Thank you so much," read the letter, which was from the rock musician. "I have never laughed this much in my whole life. But I realize that we embarrassed you, so to make up for this, I am paying for your hotel room. We wish you a happy journey and thank you for the joy and laughter you brought to us."

The Swedish couple learned that sometimes fear can be overcome by love. As the musician began to laugh, love came into his heart, and it also came back to the Swedish couple. He was able to give a gift of love to the woman who had inadvertently opened his heart to love through laughter.

24. At the Grocery Store

A woman was in a grocery store at ten o'clock one night with her husband and children. They had gotten behind in their shopping because their car and their truck had been in the repair shop. So the whole family was getting groceries for the week.

The woman had the shopping cart quite full by the time she reached the checkout counter. It was late at night for the young children to be out, and the woman was tired and wanted to get home. They had chosen this store because it usually offered very quick service, but that evening there was a brand-new checker working. He was very slow.

The young man seemed unsure of how to run the register. A supervisor came up behind him and gave him instructions for a while but then had to leave. Finally the line moved forward, and the young man began checking the family's groceries.

He picked up an item that had to be priced. He started to look it up, but he didn't know what it was. "It's an avocado," she told him. He punched the wrong code into the machine, and it registered as broccoli. Unable to figure out how to fix the error and get the computer to price the correct item, he just stood there, helpless. Soon the supervisor came back and corrected the computer to the price for avocado. The minutes ticked by as the checker moved along his very slow and painful course.

The children were helping bag the groceries, but the young checker was so slow that the children just stood at the end of the counter, waiting for the food to come down the belt so they could put it in the bags. The husband finally decided to go outside and sit in the car because there was nothing else for him to do.

The woman felt very tired, but watching the young checker she suddenly had compassion and understanding for him. She realized that on top of his confusion he didn't need a customer who was angry or upset.

The woman realized that this young man needed love and understanding more than she needed to rest. And in giving love and compassion to him in the things he didn't know, she found herself filled with love. Much of the tiredness she had felt coming into the store was now gone.

It's funny how this divine principle of the Holy Spirit works. Often we feel so tired that we wonder if we can take even one more step. In our mind is the answer: We need rest. We need someone to rub our shoulders. But the Holy Spirit might have quite a different solution.

As we give of ourselves, of our patience and love, to someone else who needs it more, something changes inside us. Something flows in, a flow of good feeling. A spiritual upliftment oc-

curs both in us and in the person receiving the
love.

25. The Piano Player

A man played the piano at a Methodist church. At weddings and celebrations, he usually played his own compositions, happy songs that fit within the religious framework. As an ECKist, he had many reasons for not attending the Methodist services, but he found the people were very open to the Light and Sound of God through his playing.

He and his wife had just returned from vacation, and they were feeling especially good. He hadn't played the piano in several weeks, and his first service back was a funeral. He wasn't particularly happy about it, but it was part of his job.

He arrived at the church about twenty-five minutes before the service to warm up a little. The deceased woman had had many close friends in the church. Sorrow and grief hung in the air; the emotions felt very heavy. The ECKist worked hard to shake off the heaviness so he could be clear in his playing. Although you can't get too happy at a funeral, he tried to keep the music as light and enjoyable as possible.

He played several popular tunes in the prelude, then a few pieces during the service for the soloist. His ending piece had an upbeat, happy tone. He felt good because, although it had been several weeks since he had last played, he had done well.

He didn't know the full effect of his music until the next Sunday. A man came up to him; it was the widower. "Before the service began last week," he said, "my stomach was all in knots. I hurt so badly inside that I didn't trust myself to speak. But as you played, I felt the hurt being released, and I began to feel better." He added, "By the end of the service, I even felt as if I might be able to go back out and face the world."

Like the piano player, many ECKists give of themselves by being of service to others, doing the things that bring the Light and Sound of God to other people, even though the others are unaware of it.

Unless the members of a spiritual teaching carry something spiritual and uplifting into the world, they become an introverted group. We have to go out into the world. We have to give of ourselves—not in an emotional way, but as true service to others, in the way they need at the moment. We give others not what we think they need but what they really need, as Divine Spirit directs us.

26. The Holiness of the Moment

While staying in another city for an ECK seminar, I found myself eating dinner at the same restaurant several nights in a row. I am always on the lookout for people who are happy and living in the present moment, and I happened to notice a young woman working there.

This person did a number of jobs in the restaurant. One evening, she was working as the hostess, seating people who came in. I was struck by how well she did her job. She did everything she could to make the customers comfortable.

The next evening she was working behind the serving line of the food buffet. Several other young women were there, chatting about their social lives and having a good time.

The girls were too busy discussing their social lives to have any time for the customers, but this one young woman I had seen earlier was ready to help. She explained what certain foods were; she went to a lot of trouble just to make sure the customers would understand what they would be getting.

This young person seemed to recognize that this present moment is a holy, sacred occasion. I look for people like this, who enjoy what they're doing at the moment, no matter what it is. Some work as hair stylists and create works of art from other people's hair problems. The customer just sees the tangled hair, but in the expert stylist's eyes there is possibility there, waiting to be made beautiful.

A person who lives in the holiness of the moment is always looking for the potential of whatever that moment may bring. Always.

27. The Decorated Bus

A woman worked as a bus driver for children in special-education classes. Many of the children had very definite emotional problems that often stemmed from family difficulties. Their fights at school had become such a problem that the school authorities had put them in their own special classes. In a sense, they had become the castoffs of their school.

Other children made fun of them because they had to ride in a special little bus that was smaller and plainer than the regular vehicles. So when the Christmas season came, the bus driver decided to do something special for these children. She bought garlands and other Christmas decorations and hung them inside the bus. She made it just as pretty as she could, then she drove to the bus stop where the children would get on. She couldn't wait to see their expressions when they noticed the bus.

These were tough children who had been through a lot. But they got on the bus almost reverently and didn't allow anyone to tear down their decorations. They said to each other, "We have a special bus. Leave the decorations up!"

When the other children came by and looked at the decorated bus, they became envious. They went to their bus drivers and asked, "When are you going to decorate *our* bus?"

The bus driver's gift to the special-education children was an expression of the divine love of one Soul for others. Perhaps later in life these children will grow up and become leaders in some area of society. Not all of them will, but some might remember that special bus, decorated as a gift of love.

A gift of true love is always God's love to you that you give to another.

28. Yellow Marigolds

The growing season was about over, but I wanted to buy some flowers to put around my yard. I drove to a nursery to see if they had any left. The parking lot was empty. I thought, They probably have sold everything. I wonder if I'll be able to find a flower? But I walked over to the greenhouse to see.

I started to slide open the greenhouse door when a checkout clerk appeared. "Customers are not allowed in the greenhouse area," she said abruptly. I thought, Whoa! I'm a peace-loving person; all I want is some flowers. I didn't come for a fight.

So I quickly slid the door shut and walked into the main building. There were a few leftover pots of flowers there, ones that they hadn't sold during the season. I stood by them, debating over whether I should buy one or just leave to avoid the rude clerk.

All of a sudden there was a commotion at the front door. A man slammed down a potted tree that looked very dead. He was angry and cursing. Who does he run into but the rude clerk?

"I want my money back," he said, very upset, "or I want you to give me another tree. This tree is dead."

"We don't give returns," the clerk replied coldly. "We don't know what kind of care you gave the tree after we sold it to you." She stood there staring at the man, jaw to jaw.

I mentally flipped a coin, wondering who I'd put my money on in a fistfight. I thought the man would win, because he was bigger and madder. She had it coming, I thought. But a cat-and-dog fight could spoil a perfectly good day. So I began singing HU really quietly inside myself. I was trying to make myself totally clear; I wasn't trying to stop a fight.

The clerk suddenly came to her senses: This man was seriously angry, and she could very well get a bloody nose. "I'm going to get my supervisor," she said quickly and ran into the back room.

The supervisor was a much younger woman and very calm. She stepped over to the angry man and smiled up at him. "What can I do for you?" she asked. "I bought this tree, and it died," the man said. "I'm sure we can work something out," the supervisor said pleasantly, and they walked out to look at the tree that was still in the doorway.

"This happens sometimes," she said. "But the season's over, and we just don't have any more trees. I do have some hanging plants. They're about the same price as the tree you bought. If you'd like one of them, you can have your choice. There are several different price ranges; you can have the most expensive."

The man calmed down right away. "That seems fair," he said. The rude clerk saw that everything was smoothing out, and this irritated her. "You let that tree die," she shot at the man.

"Shut up or I'm going to hit you," the man shot back. This subdued the clerk who realized he still had his punch. She went back to the checkout counter and stood there, meek as a lamb. The man chose a plant, took it directly to the door, and left a few choice words with the clerk on the way out.

As I went up to the checkout counter, I saw that the clerk was actually shaking. The man's violent anger had really upset her. "That was tough," I said sympathetically. She looked at me with relief and very nicely said, "Could I help you find something?"

"I was looking for some marigolds," I said, "but I wanted yellow flowers. All I saw were bronze ones."

"We have some more marigolds in the back," she said. "They're closer to yellow than bronze." She took me to the greenhouse, and I picked out a few pots.

"And what kind of hanging plants do you have?" I asked.

"I just pruned these," she said. "I'll let you have one for the price of the cheaper ones." Then as she was ringing up my purchases, she threw in the marigolds for free.

Because I was sympathetic to her, she gave me a gift back. She probably didn't realize that she was involved in the gift of spiritual giving.

These things happen in life all the time. It's the state of consciousness that we have and carry with us that makes this life heaven or hell.

29. Flowers for Mahanta

A Nigerian ECKist occasionally traveled to South America on business. He and other businessmen stayed at one particular hotel, but the youngest sister of the hotelier had a strong prejudice against colored people, especially blacks. Whenever this group of black businessmen came to this hotel, she was very rude to them.

On one particular trip, the businessman was thinking about his love for the Mahanta and decided he would like to buy flowers for the Mahanta if he could.

So he asked the Inner Master, "Can I buy flowers for you?"

The Master said, "Buy them for yourself." But the man answered, "I cannot buy them for myself, because that would be selfish."

"Buy them anyway," said the Mahanta.

On Sunday morning the shops were usually closed, except for a fruit market. The man went there to get some apples, then he saw a boy outside the market selling flowers. The businessman bought two roses and took them back to the hotel.

As he looked at the roses, he felt an inner nudge to touch the flowers to his heart. Immediately he felt the warm love of the Mahanta when the roses touched him. He almost cried with the sheer love and joy he felt. Then he heard the

Master say, "Because you were willing to buy these flowers, you were showing me that you were willing to open your heart to me."

Now the ECKist had two very special roses. He wondered if he should give them to his fellow businessmen. Would they even appreciate the gift?

He took the two roses back to his hotel where he ran into the sister of the hotel owner. He said, "Good morning." She hissed back at him. So he took the two roses into the TV room and began to put them into a glass of water.

Immediately the woman's manner changed from cold to warm. "Are those flowers for me?" she smiled.

"No, they're for everybody," the ECKist answered. "Well, let me help you put them in water," said the woman.

For the rest of their visit, the woman was very cordial to the black businessmen. One of the other men commented to the ECKist, "I've come here for three years. This is the first time she has ever spoken to me."

In wanting to be a better friend of the Mahanta, the ECKist was shown how the love of the Mahanta can reach even the hardest heart.

30. Video Tokens

I'd given someone an initiation in ECK, and they brought fruit as a gift for God. There is never a charge for an initiation in ECK, but people sometimes show their love for God through giving the Initiator fruit or flowers.

Besides the fruit, this person pulled out a handful of coins. "Here are some video tokens I brought for you. These are for you personally."

I wanted to go to the video arcade, cash the tokens in, and give the money to ECKANKAR, because I felt that would've been the right thing to do. But the person looked at me and said, "These are nonrefundable."

So I didn't know what to do with these four tokens. When I got home, I just put them in the watch pocket in my jeans where I already had one token. Now I had five. And I forgot about them.

After the dedication of the Temple of ECK in October 1990, the energy was flowing through me very strongly. I couldn't work, so I told my wife, "I'm going to run some errands and pick up the mail."

I stopped by an automatic teller machine to get some cash, but the store owner said the machine was broken. The nearest one was down the street in the video arcade. So I went to the video arcade, thinking I could burn off some of this excess energy from the dedication.

Inside I found a game I'd been playing for a while, but the buttons were sticking. So I quit and went over to Ms. Pac-Man to wait for a turn. All of a sudden I saw three people with their spiritual lights on. I can always tell the ECKists, even in a crowd. The spiritual light of ECK comes through them very strongly.

This mother and her two children caught sight of me. They were beaming. I went up to them and said hello. The mother explained that the children had gotten very good grades in school and the video arcade gave free tokens for every A a child brought home on the report card. While we were talking, the children went off to play one of the open games.

Then I saw Ms. Pac-Man was free. "Quick!" I said to the mother, "You can get Ms. Pac-Man if you move fast." "I gave my last token to my son," she said. I had also used up four of my tokens and given the fifth to her son too. So I said to her, "I'll get you some."

"No, I couldn't," she said. "It's only a dollar," I said. Then I realized this was exactly the dollar's worth of tokens I had gotten at the initiation and wanted to give back to the ECK. Here was a perfect opportunity.

I respect the ECK initiations. If money comes in, I give it to ECKANKAR because it is given as a gift for God. In the video arcade I was able to give back the tokens to the ECK by giving them to this woman. And I found the tiredness from

the excess energy was suddenly gone; I had come
alive again.

31. Buying a Suit

For four years I had looked for a new suit in the right shade of blue. En route to or from a seminar, I'd often run into a clothing store for a few minutes before flights. I thought I could find a light, uplifting shade of blue in one of the sunny areas—Florida, Hawaii, California, or Australia. But I finally found my suit here at home.

The day I bought the suit, I took it home to show my wife. I always test out the salesman by saying, "I'd like to have my wife come in and check this out before I buy." I want to buy from someone who respects a husband and wife and how they make decisions together. The salesman was very understanding about this.

"That's perfectly all right; I know how it is," he said. But because it was seminar time and we were both very busy, I went back for alterations alone.

The same salesman was there, and he began to measure the suit for alterations. "Would you like a small break in the trousers?" he said. "Yes," I said. So he pinned up the trousers. "Can you do a little more?" I said. "They look fine to me," he said.

"What about the sleeves?" he asked. "I'd like them a little longer," I said. "They look fine to me," he said. We went through the whole suit this way. The only problem was, he was the expert. Every time I had an opinion about the suit, all I got was, "Don't worry."

When I got home and showed the suit to my wife, she said, "When that man asked if you wanted a break in the trousers, he was talking a whole different language than you." "Yeah," I said, "I look like I'm standing in two gunnysacks." The salesman was an elderly gentleman, from an age when people wore their trousers very baggy.

So I took the suit to a tailor nearby. He didn't speak much English, but he knew how to tailor clothing. His family was from a Middle Eastern country, and he was a little defensive because of the war in the Persian Gulf. He felt persecuted in this country.

So he didn't say much as he pinned the suit. "Just a little break?" he asked. "Yeah, just a little break," I said. His eyes when he looked at me were very detached, businesslike. It was as if there was a very hard-hearted human being inside the skin.

But I began chatting a little with him. "It's just some wonderful rain we're having," I said. "Yes, but tomorrow it looks like it's going to be sunshine," he said. I'm talking about rain because of the drought we'd been having. He's from the Middle East, so he's more used to sunshine than rain.

As soon as we began to talk about a neutral subject, his eyes lit up and I saw the light of love there. He had the eyes of a very gentle human being, a man with humor. He finished measuring my suit and did a good job on it, so I wished him good day and left the shop.

Something I appreciate more than anything in everyday life is finding a person through whom this Light of God is shining. I feel the love that is in other people. Because of the restrictions of business and running to make appointments, people don't often feel there is time to be human, to let others know they're appreciated. But some people have an attitude that says, "I like your company. We have to do business but we might as well enjoy doing business."

People who have this attitude are open-hearted. They love their work. And through this love for their work, they are reflecting the love of God.

32. Coffee Break

One Saturday morning a woman and her husband decided to go shopping at an expensive home-furnishings store. The company was having a warehouse sale that began at 10:00 a.m. Right next to the warehouse was the regular store, which opened at 9:00 a.m.

The couple arrived about fifteen minutes before the regular store opened. Outside in the cold, unloading a furniture truck, was a young man. The couple asked him if there was a coffee shop nearby where they could wait. The young man gave them directions, and they set off.

They drove around for about ten minutes but couldn't find the coffee shop, so they came back to the warehouse. The young man was still unloading furniture. He gave them the directions again, but they thanked him and said they'd just wait inside the store.

Coming into the front of the store, the couple met a very agitated young woman. "Are you here for the warehouse sale?" she asked. The couple nodded. "Well, you'll have to wait until 10:00 a.m.," the young woman said, and shut the door in their faces. They opened the door again and asked, "Isn't this store open now?" "Well, yes," said the woman. "We'd like to look around," said the couple. And the woman said OK.

They wandered through the store, looking at

the very expensive rugs and furniture. Then the young man came in, carrying two cups of coffee. "I know you didn't get your coffee," he said. "I thought you might like some." The couple thanked him and started sipping.

Immediately the young woman came running out from the back room. "Coffee isn't allowed in here," she said to the young man. Turning to the couple, she said, "If you want to drink that coffee, you'll have to drink it outside."

It was winter, and the wife looked out at the snow. Normally this was the point where she and her husband and the salesperson would have all lost their tempers, she thought. But she said very kindly, "I can understand how you feel. We also have a home with very many expensive furnishings. But we know how to drink coffee so that we don't spill it all over. You can trust us. We won't do it here."

The young woman was still upset and said some rather unkind things in return. The wife answered, "I think it's bad business to criticize an employee like the truck driver who serves a customer even though it isn't store rules. He made us feel welcome."

The young woman finally apologized. "My dog's been sick, and I haven't slept much," she explained, and went into the back of the store.

The wife and her husband walked around looking at the furniture and drinking their coffee. They could overhear the young woman talking to an elderly man in the back of the store.

"I don't even know if I should be at work today," she was saying, telling the man about how sick her dog was. She didn't know if the dog would get better, and she was so worried.

Then the wife came over to the young woman. "I couldn't help overhearing," she said. "I can understand how you must feel. I have a cat now, but I used to have a dog. We love our pets as much as we would love a child."

The young woman stood up, and the two women spontaneously hugged each other. The saleswoman said, "I have to apologize for my rude behavior before. I feel so bad. I guess I just have to chill out."

"Well, you could have a coffee and drink it outside," the ECKist said, laughing. Fortunately the young woman had gotten her sense of humor back and laughed at the joke.

The ECKist was showing the saleswoman some of the riches of ECK, what she had gotten inwardly in the form of love from the Holy Spirit. Instead of flying off the handle at the saleswoman's attitude, she decided the rude behavior wasn't going to spoil her Saturday morning.

Because the ECKist waited around and kept looking, she heard more of the story. She learned that this young woman had some problems that affected her and hurt her very much. Eventually she was able to give her love and understanding.

Contemplations . . .

Our purpose in ECKANKAR is to become a Co-worker with God. If we are helping others in their spiritual unfoldment—in ECK or outside ECKANKAR—we are Co-workers with God.

* * *

To receive love sounds easy enough, but many people have a hard time accepting it from others. This is apparent when someone responds to a gift by saying, "I can't take that." If you were to suggest that their attitude was due to their inability to accept love, they would only deny it. But actions speak louder than words.

* * *

Soul moves through the evolutionary process in a number of different forms, including those of animals and birds. These are some of the many different ways in which Soul gains experience, thereby gaining expression of Its divine self. In the process, Soul must learn to receive love and to give love.

* * *

As we give of ourselves, of our patience and love, to someone else who needs it more, something changes inside us. Something flows in, a flow of good feeling. There is a spiritual upliftment that occurs both in us and in the person receiving the love.

* * *

Unless the members of a spiritual teaching carry something spiritual and uplifting into the world, they become an introverted group. We have to go out into the world. We have to give of ourselves—not in an emotional way, but as true service to others, in the way they need at the moment. We give others not what we think they need but what they really need, as Divine Spirit directs us.

Children love to sing HU because it is the sound in everything. If you sing it, you'll be shown a way to see the HU as it manifests in the activities of people around you.

Chapter Four

HU, a Love Song to God

33. Sound of HU

A mother picked up her three-year-old son from nursery school one day. The teacher came out to meet her.

"What is this 'HU-ee' song your son sings?" the teacher asked. "The children had been restless and uncooperative all day, but a little while ago your son began singing this 'HU-ee' song, and the children settled down. They're better now than they've been all day."

The mother didn't quite know what to say. "My little boy does spiritual exercises with the family each evening. We sing HU together," she began.

"What is HU?" the teacher asked.

"It's a love song to God. It's nondenominational, anyone can sing it" the mother explained. Just at that moment her little boy ran out to meet her, and they left.

Children love to sing HU because it is the sound in everything. If you sing it, you'll be shown a way to see the HU as it manifests in the activities of people around you.

34. Feeding the Ducks

A staff worker at the ECKANKAR Spiritual Center often walked to a nearby pond on her breaks.

The ducks would come up to her and just watch her, as she quitely sang HU, a love song to God. The ducks seemed to like it. When she walked along the shore, they waddled after her as fast as they could.

One day she decided to bring the ducks some popcorn. This time when she walked toward them, they all swam away. They wouldn't come out of the water. She threw the popcorn at them, but they didn't even eat it. She was very disappointed.

A few days later, the ECKist came back to the pond with some whole-grain bread. Two large geese were sitting by the water. But when she approached them with the bread, they flew into the pond and swam away from her. Nobody wanted her food.

As she was walking away, a thought struck her. Other people were giving the ducks and geese love in the form of food, love reduced down to a material substance. The ducks and geese had simply wanted a purer love, which she had been giving them by singing HU.

She learned a lesson from this. Birds and animals need love as much as we humans do. She could give it to all life through the love song to God, the HU.

35. Unexpected Rescue

A Catholic man in his early thirties was having a hard time sleeping at night. He had a recurring nightmare where he was both a participant and an observer at the same time. It frightened him because he had no idea of what was happening.

The Catholic man had heard about the word *HU* from one of his friends who is an ECKist. They had gone to a twelve-step program together, and this friend had told him, "Whenever you have a problem and you don't know what to do, just sing HU silently to yourself. It's a sacred name for God."

That night the dream came again. He was in a barnyard with a strange creature. It had a snake's body, a head like a turkey, and dark blue coloring.

This creature came up to the dreamer and begin conversing. Somehow the man knew he had to tap the turkey-headed snake on the forehead with his fingers every few moments to keep from being harmed. So every few minutes he reached out his hand and tapped the ghastly looking creature on its head.

The Catholic man knew he was asleep in bed yet the dream was so real. He was terribly frightened because he couldn't wake up. Then he remembered what his ECKist friend had said:

When you're in trouble, sing HU.

In the middle of the nightmare the man began singing HU. Suddenly the whole scene—the barnyard, the turkey-headed snake, everything—just vanished into midair. The man woke with a pounding heart. He knew he wasn't as afraid anymore.

Sleep came again, and the man found himself in the barnyard with the turkey-headed snake once more. What do I do now? he wondered, and right away he knew to just sing HU. Again, the scene disappeared.

The Catholic man told his friend about the dream and thanked him. He was very grateful that the secret name of God was available for people of all religions to use. He explained that the prayers he knew as a Catholic were much too long and complicated to remember in a dream. But HU was simple; he could remember HU.

36. Sanctity of Consciousness

A nurse who is the mother of two tiny daughters took them shopping in a mall about an hour's drive from their house. On the way home, the girls fell asleep in the back seat. The nurse remembered that she needed to stop for some groceries, but she didn't want to wake the children.

Forty minutes from home, she had a very strong nudge from the ECK, the Holy Spirit, to stop at a particular food store, even though there were many food stores closer to her house. She woke her two babies and took them inside, got her groceries, and paid for them.

As she was leaving, an elderly woman in front of her suddenly fell to the floor. Panic erupted among the shoppers. The unconscious woman's daughter began to scream, and a man yelled, "Someone get an ambulance!"

The nurse put her two children in a shopping cart where they'd be safe. She knelt beside the unconscious woman's daughter who was sitting on the floor, cradling her mother's head in her arms. "I'm a nurse," the ECKist said. "What can I do to help?"

"Please hold my mother's head so I can turn off the ignition," said the daughter. Her car was parked in front, and the motor was still running.

So the nurse sat down on the floor with the

unconscious woman in her arms and her two daughters in the shopping cart nearby. Everyone was still in a panic. To calm the situation, the nurse began to softly sing HU, a sacred name of God.

After she had sung HU about six times, the elderly woman's eyes suddenly snapped open. The woman looked into the nurse's eyes; and the ECKist knew suddenly that the woman, as Soul, was looking at her. To the nurse, it seemed like the moment of spiritual awakening for this elderly woman who had fallen.

Pretty soon others came, and the nurse was free to return to her children. Later, telling a friend about the incident, she realized she had chanted HU only to bring stability to herself and to the situation. She had not tried to use HU to make the woman better or invade her consciousness in any way. The nurse knew the sanctity of another person's state of consciousness, even if that person was unconscious.

When you sing the name of God, HU, never use it to change another's mind or another's will. Don't use it to change their state of health, because that person is what he or she is. To change or try to change them in this way is wrong.

37. The HU Book

When a boy was six years old, his parents—both ECKists—were divorced. Before the divorce, the entire family had practiced the spiritual exercises together and used the word *HU*. So the boy had grown up singing HU, often seeing the Inner Master.

After the divorce, the boy and his mother moved to a different town, where the mother met a man from another culture and religion. The mother and this man eventually got married.

The stepfather tried to stop the boy from singing HU. The stepfather followed a very rigid, intolerant religion. He had no room to love anyone who believed something other than his beliefs.

He tried to break the connection the boy had with the path of ECK. But the boy knew the Light and Sound of God, and the Blue Star of the Mahanta, and he continued to travel on the inner planes at night. Meanwhile, the stepfather cleared all the ECK material out of the home.

The boy had a grandmother who was also in ECK. When the boy came to visit his grandmother one day, he asked her over and over again, "Where is my HU book? Let's go look for my HU book." So the boy and his grandmother combed the bookstores and libraries, but they could never find the HU book the boy was talking about.

About a year later, a book was published by

ECKANKAR about the HU. When the grandmother saw it at the local ECK Center, she thought she could buy it for the boy without offending the stepfather. The whole family was coming over for a visit, but before they arrived, she decided to hide the book because she was afraid of causing offense. She put the book in her bookcase behind the other books.

When the family arrived, immediately the grandson said, "Where's my HU book?" And he walked straight to the bookcase, pulled out the books in front, and found the book his grandmother had bought.

"Here it is," he said. "Here's my HU book."

The boy had seen the book a year before on the inner planes. His connection with the Living ECK Master was very strong, built upon the Light and Sound of God.

38. Mr. Caruthers

For a while I was meeting a man on the inner planes who reminded me a bit of Joseph Campbell, the noted mythologist who translated a few years ago. This gentleman had presence and bearing about him. He was probably eighty in terms of earth years.

We met every day. He was interested in ECK, especially in HU and the Light and Sound. He wanted to know more about these things. We'd meet, sit, and talk about ECK, but we'd never exchanged names.

One day I was on the inner planes in an office building. I was there to talk with some businessmen about ECK. In the reception area was a buffet table set with very lavish food. It looked as if guests were about to arrive.

At the other end of the room was a conference table where ten members of the board of directors were sitting. They all had very surprised looks on their faces. I learned they had just found out about the passing of one of their fellow directors—a Mr. Caruthers. Nobody knew his background, but he had been a constant presence on the board, often giving his wisdom and his knowledge. Now they had learned he'd translated, or died, and they didn't know what to make of it.

As we talked, an idea suddenly struck me. I asked them, "Do you have any photographs of

Mr. Caruthers?" They showed me a very old photo. It was a younger version of the man I had secretly called Mr. HU. I realized that he and I had been meeting because he needed to hear about the HU and the Light and Sound. This was the tool, or lesson, he needed in order to progress to the next higher spiritual level.

Translation also occurs on the inner planes. We like to think we go from the physical body into the inner planes and stay there. But people also translate on the inner planes of the spiritual worlds. At some time, they too will move into higher levels of existence.

39. My Name Is HU

The dean of a college was on her way to attend a refresher course that administrators took to brush up on their skills. The trainer for the group came to meet the ECKist at the airport. As they were driving to the hotel, the trainer unexpectedly confided that she had been ill for the last couple of months. "Despite what the doctors say, I believe there is a spiritual reason for my illness," she said. "I want to know what it is." At such an unexpected turn in the conversation, the ECKist saw that the weekend had taken on a spiritual tone.

About fifteen people were at the training. They were chief executives of colleges all over the country. Very educated people, they ranged in age from thirty-five to sixty-five.

As an icebreaker, the trainer asked them to sit in a large circle. "First give your name," the trainer said, "then tell the group how you think the world perceives you." The first person said, "My name is John, and I think the world sees me as a rather broad-minded educator." And they went around the group.

Then the trainer said, "Now sing your name, your real name, three times." In other words, someone whose name was Mary might say, "I feel my real name is actually Melanie," and she would sing *Melanie* three times. Then the whole group would sing *Melanie* three times too.

Finally it was the ECKist's turn. When asked about her real identity, "I am Spirit," she said. "I listen for the Sound and I look for the Light, even though this may not show in my business clothes." Then she said, "My real name is HU. That is the name of God. It's not that I am God, but I can become Godlike." And she began to sing the word *HU* three times.

Then all the administrators began to sing HU right along with her. The ECKist thought it was quite something, a business meeting where everyone was singing HU.

Afterward people came up to her and wanted to know more. "What is HU?" they asked. "What is ECKANKAR and ECK?" All weekend long, the ECKist got to explain what ECKANKAR was.

40. The Peaceful Parrot

A man had a temperamental parrot. When he bought it, the parrot was a quiet bird who would sit on his perch and watch the family. But when the parrot got into one of its bad moods, it would carry on, squawking and making all kinds of noise, being a real pest to the household. No one could get any rest from the parrot's squawking.

The owner happened to be an ECKist. "We can't put up with the bad habits of our parrot anymore," he said one day to his wife. "What if we chanted HU? Not to change the parrot, but perhaps to open the way for ECK to bring whatever It wants into the household."

The family sat down and began chanting HU. Suddenly the parrot stopped squawking. It became very quiet and docile.

After that the household returned to a peaceful setting. The parrot remained good-natured, and whenever it got into a bad mood after that, the owner would chant HU. Sometimes the parrot would join in.

In our human way, we feel we are God's special creation, and animals and birds are not. But Soul in some of Its earlier forms of experience may take on the body of a bird as easily as It would take on the body of a human being.

41. The Song That Makes God Happy

A woman and her six-year-old daughter liked to do a spiritual exercise each night before the little girl went to sleep. They sat on the bed together and sang HU.

Sometimes the little girl would break into random singing or chattering about this or that. And the mother wondered, Does my child really understand what HU is all about?

One night the little girl turned to her mother and said, "I know why we sing HU."

Surprised, the mother asked, "Why?"

"Because it's the song that makes God happy," the child said. "It brings up all His joys. It's the song of the spirit of life."

Children speak from their hearts. Perhaps the terminology doesn't always follow what we'd find in the ECK books. We speak of God, the SUGMAD, as IT rather than he or she. IT is above the qualities of negative and positive. But in our human language we actually can't even begin to approach the concept of God, except to talk about ITS qualities of love.

All that we can possibly do with the word HU is sing it and give it reverence. It represents the love of God for Soul, and we are Soul. HU represents the enormous love the Creator has for ITS creation.

42. HU for All You Do

Money was short for a certain African man, and he didn't really have enough to buy food for his family. His hobby was fishing, and he decided to see if he could catch something so his family could have a meal or two.

He got on a bus late that night and went out to a lagoon. When he got there, he put on a heavy suit to ward off mosquitoes and keep himself warm. After he fished for a while and caught enough for his family, he sat on the sand for a few minutes resting before he caught the bus home.

Suddenly he saw a tall man coming along the beach. The moon peeked out for a minute, and he saw something glinting at the man's side. The tall man approached him and said, "My friend, what are you doing here at night?"

The ECKist saw the man had a long knife in a scabbard and it was glinting in the moonlight although the stranger had it hidden a little in back of him. So the ECKist began to chant HU quietly inside himself, and he didn't answer.

The stranger thought, Well, this fisherman must not speak English. He tried one of the native languages, but still the ECKist didn't respond. So the stranger tried again in English.

"I am here fishing with my friends," said the ECKist finally.

"That's strange," said the tall stranger. "Before I came up to you, I looked all over. I saw no people anywhere. Where are your friends?"

And the ECKist said, "Over there." He pointed off in the dark down the beach.

The man said, "I don't see anyone."

"Well, look again," said the ECKist. And he kept chanting HU.

Suddenly the tall man started counting, "One. Two." He was counting people coming through the night not far off down the beach. The ECKist looked over and saw two people walking toward them.

Then the tall man said, "Three, four."And the ECKist also saw two more people. Suddenly there weren't just four people coming toward them but a whole crowd of people coming along the beach. "There they are," said the ECKist.

The tall man looked around quickly, backed a few steps away, and saw the people still coming. Then he took to his heels and sped off into the night.

The ECKist looked at the people coming down the beach, and suddenly they melted away into nothingness. They just disappeared. Then he realized what he had so often heard from the Mahanta, the Living ECK Master: "You are not alone. I am always with you."

The ECKist was protected because he sang the name of God, HU. You don't have to be an ECKist to sing HU. You can sing HU when you are in trouble, as the fisherman did. It's a love song to God, a connection between Soul and the Divine Being.

If you really care about finding truth, sing HU.

Contemplations . . .

If you're asked or if you ever feel the occasion is right, tell people about the HU. Tell them, "Sing HU, maybe it can heal your heart."

* * *

What is HU? It is a very holy name for God. In it are contained all sounds.

* * *

When you sing HU, know that this is one of the most sacred names for God. Sing it with love and with reverence. Look for the Light, listen for the Sound. It'll give you spiritual insight, but it doesn't come overnight. You have to develop it like any other skill.

* * *

The presence of the Temple of ECK on earth will begin to make it easier for people to say they are ECKists and to share the HU with others in all kinds of settings.

* * *

When you sing the name of God, HU, never use it to change another's mind or another's will. Don't use it to change their state of health, because that person is what he or she is. To change or try to change them in this way is wrong.

* * *

People singing softly to each other, the song is of the HU. People laughing, the laughter is of the HU. And even when there are people crying, the crying is of the HU. The falling rain, its sound is of the HU. And the birds, and the wind. These are all of the sound of HU.

* * *

HU represents the enormous love the Creator has for ITS creation.

So often in our spiritual unfoldment, we are like the alchemist. We want to make the big leap. We want a shortcut. We will work so hard at the shortcut that unless there is someone with common sense—like the Dream Master—to help us get back in balance, we waste our time.

Chapter Five

Family
and Relationships

43. Raising Bananas

An old man had a lovely young daughter. The daughter married a handsome young student. They were very happy in all ways except one: The student was very impractical.

The student was an alchemist. He thought that if he studied long and hard enough, he could find the secret of turning base material into gold.

The old man felt very bad that his daughter had married such an individual—someone who had no sense about how to make his living in the world. So the old man thought of a way that he might address the problem.

He called his young son-in-law into his home one day. The old man very carefully shut all the windows and doors. Then he turned to the young man.

"I hear you are an alchemist," he said.

"Yes, I am," said the young man.

"I am too," replied his father-in-law. "But I have found the secret."

"You did?" the young man exclaimed.

The old man said, "Yes. And I'll teach it to you too. On the bottom of a banana leaf is a fine, silvery powder. You have to scrape this off and collect it. It takes a very long time to gather even an ounce, and you'll need five pounds of this silvery powder before you can turn base material into gold."

The young man said he would do it.

The years went by, and the student was still growing bananas and very carefully scraping the silvery dust from the bottom of the leaves. After many years, the young man and his wife came back to the old man.

"I've got five pounds of the silver dust," he said.

"Very good," he said. "But what did you do with the bananas?" he asked his daughter.

"I sold them so we could live," replied the daughter.

"Do you have any savings?" asked her father.

"Oh, yes," she said. And she put a bag of gold on the table. "I sold the bananas all these years and used the money wisely. Now we have this bag of gold."

The old man got a handful of dirt and put it beside the bag of gold. "Base material into gold," he said.

So often in our spiritual unfoldment, we are like the alchemist. We want to make the big leap. We want a shortcut. We will work so hard at the shortcut that unless there is someone with common sense—like the Dream Master—to help us get back in balance, we waste our time.

The raising of bananas brought the gold. The silver dust on the bottom of the leaves had nothing to do with it, except that it was the silver dust of inspiration.

44. Showing Compassion

A woman had been very active in ECK. Her husband wasn't an ECKist, but he loved her and supported her activities in ECK. And then he died. Because of his death she was very lonesome. It even meant moving out of the family home.

During her time of sorrow her former friends in ECKANKAR didn't come to offer a shoulder for her to cry on. They weren't there to listen to her if she needed them. They were probably afraid they would take on her karma.

She wrote to me, "Isn't there any compassion in ECKANKAR?"

I replied in a letter, "There is compassion in ECK. Many ECKists live lives of love and compassion." But she was in very painful times and couldn't see this.

Later she understood that the lesson was for her to learn tolerance. She decided she couldn't criticize these people who were practicing what they thought was complete detachment. "But was the Good Samaritan of the Bible wrong?" she asked.

"Of course not," I wrote. "The power of love is always stronger than the fear of karma." If someone had showed her a little love and compassion, maybe it would've healed her weeping heart a little sooner.

The old, lopsided consciousness of individuality that was in ECKANKAR expressed itself in this woman's experience. Just listening to someone in pain is acting as a Co-worker with God. You can do this right at home in your own family.

45. Walking the Dog

One very hot summer evening I had just finished mowing the lawn and was setting up the
hose to water my flowers. I have geraniums lined
up along the driveway. They're pretty colors—
white, pink, and red—and they greet me when I
come home. And when the neighbors come by,
the flowers make them happy too. People often
stop to tell me how pretty the flowers are.

That afternoon a neighbor was out walking
his dog and stopped by to chat. "Your flowers are
so pretty," he said. And I said, "Plants need love
just like animals, just like your dog."

This seemed to catch him off guard. I imagined he had just come home from work and
probably the last thing he wanted to do was take
the dog for a walk. But on this very hot evening
here was this man being led down the block by
his huge dog.

The man looked down at his dog as if to say,
"Excuse me for being so rude. I understand why
you must have your walk. Let's go." And they
continued on their way down the street.

It hadn't even occurred to me while I was
speaking that this man may have been a little
annoyed at having to take his dog for a walk just
then. But this was part of a waking dream for
him. He was getting a lesson on how to treat his
pet better. Something in meeting with a neighbor

had awakened him to be more conscious of what he was doing in his daily chores.

This is part of the universal nature of dreams—our daily waking life. It goes beyond the drudgery of chores we've done before, where we've gone to sleep spiritually.

It was very important for that man to walk his dog at that particular time, and it was very important for me to care for my geraniums just then.

46. Lunch Break

A teacher in Sweden was in charge of young children in a public school. Lately she had been noticing the children quarreling among themselves; they seemed less happy than usual. And she wondered what she could do about it.

So one evening she went into contemplation and asked the Mahanta to show her if there was some way to help the children get along better. That night she had a dream. The Inner Master came to her and said, "Talk about the happy things in class."

The next day after lunch break, the teacher sat down with the children. "How many of you had a good time on lunch break today?" she asked. A number of hands went up. So she asked each of these children what they had done to make their lunch break a happy one. Some had jumped rope, some had played marbles, and some had played tag or another game.

When all these children spoke of their happy times at lunch, it left an impression on the children who didn't have a happy time. Then the teacher asked, "Who didn't enjoy themselves during lunch break?"

A smaller number of hands went up, and she asked them what had happened. Some of them said they were unhappy because someone had pushed them or hit them. The teacher then took the aggressor child and the victim child into another room, and she talked with them to find out why this happened. It was one reason or another.

Then the teacher said, "If you love someone would you do this to them?" She talked some more with the children. "Now can we be friends?" she asked them. And if the two agreed, they went back into the classroom with the other children.

As she spent more time talking with the children, they got along better and quarreled less. After a few days other teachers came to her and said, "The children in your classroom are behaving much better than our children. What are you doing?" And the ECKist was able to give this simple technique of discussing the children's lunch break with them.

This is an example of an enlightened person. She went to the source of wisdom within her and got what she needed to help her solve some of her everyday problems. You can do the same.

47. Law Student's Vacation

A young couple who lived in Washington, D.C., were trying to decide about the husband's future. The wife was helping him through undergraduate school and wanted him to pursue a legal education in graduate school. But the husband couldn't decide.

The couple were going on a vacation to Massachusetts. "Why don't we look for symbols on our trip to see if we can somehow make a decision and find out what you are to do?" the wife asked. So the husband agreed.

They were visiting Concord, Massachusetts, and came to a small museum. When they were paying their entrance fee, the clerk said, "It's cheaper if you have a student discount." The couple was trying to economize wherever they could.

"You're still a student, remember?" the wife nudged her husband. He brought out his student card to show the clerk.

"Oh, you're from Georgetown University," the clerk said. "There are two other people in here right now from Georgetown University." The ECKist looked at the guest register; one name was familiar. It was one of his law professors, a favorite teacher who had always been able to inspire him.

The man and his wife walked through the museum and found the professor. The professor and a friend from England had just flown in the day before. The group had a nice chat.

Later the man said, "This was a waking dream. What are the chances that the four of us would bump into each other in this little museum in a small town far from home? I think it's a sign from the ECK about what to do with my future." The wife was happy for her husband.

The ECK can work in subtle ways, but you have to remember to ask. Most people can't hear. In ECK, you learn how to listen and see these messages from the Holy Spirit that come to you and everyone every day.

48. Air Conditioning

A couple had a very old dog who was about seventeen. She was very sensitive to temperature changes. This was a challenge where the couple lived. The summers were very hot, and the winters were very cold.

One morning when the man got up, it was already warm and muggy. He thought the day was going to get hotter, so he turned on the air conditioner. A few minutes later his wife came in.

"Don't turn that on today, dear," she said. "Yesterday I had it on and the dog started to catch a cold." The dog's health was so fragile that the temperature had to be within about a three-degree span to keep her comfortable. The wife actually spent most of the day checking the thermostat.

Catching a cold is very bad for an old dog. So the man turned the air conditioner off.

His wife went into the bathroom to clean up. "That's strange," she said, calling to her husband. "The bathroom fan just turned itself on. I wonder what that means."

Just then their little dog walked into the room. The couple looked down at the dog and got the message.

"It was too hot for the dog, I guess," said the man.

Because the bathroom fan turned on all by itself, which it had never done before, the couple knew that the ECK was trying to tell them something: Turn on the air conditioning. It'll be hot today and the dog will get too warm.

49. Listening to a Neighbor

A Higher Initiate had a neighbor who liked to talk with her about relationships. She'd go on and on about them, telling about all the problems she had.

One day the Higher Initiate was listening to her neighbor going over the same old problems. The ECKist was short on patience that day. She just wanted to get this dull cycle over with. So instead of listening, she began to offer advice from what she thought was her very high state of consciousness.

Soon the ECKist noticed something peculiar. The more they talked, the sicker she felt. She got weaker and weaker until she was unable to continue the conversation. "Excuse me," she said to her neighbor, "I just have to go lie down. I can't talk anymore."

The woman was sick all night. Her bones ached so terribly, and she couldn't get any rest. She got up and decided to listen to an ECK tape: the first one she picked was the dramatization of *The Wind of Change.*

Each story seemed to be talking about the Law of Noninterference. She realized it was a personal message for her.

By trying to give advice to her neighbor when her neighbor hadn't asked for it, she was actually taking on the karma of the other person. This is what caused her sickness.

As soon as she realized this, she went into contemplation. "I'm going to make believe that I am just listening to my neighbor," the Higher Initiate told the Inner Master. "I'm not going to offer advice; I'm just going to give charity and divine love." She envisioned the whole conversation of yesterday and how she should have done it. And just that quickly the aching in her bones went away, and she slept peacefully for the rest of the night.

When people interfere with each other, they are not expressing divine love. How many people today do this constantly? Even we in ECK don't always realize that when we violate the Law of Noninterference we are doing so because of a lack of love.

50. A Teacher's Lesson

A young Swedish girl had become very melancholy after the death of her grandmother. Her schoolteacher noticed the sadness and tried to help, but the girl couldn't seem to get over this feeling of great loss.

One afternoon the mother dropped her daughter off at school. The girl ran into the building with a happy smile on her face. The mother asked the teacher about this sudden change from sadness to happiness in the child's attitude.

Then the teacher told the mother what had happened the day before. In the classroom the children had been learning about religions. In Sweden this is allowed, as long as the religion is taught as a historical fact. The school guidelines allowed the children to write letters to a living master or a living personality and ask questions about the religion.

The teacher was an ECKist, but she had found it very difficult over the years to talk about ECKANKAR. When the children asked her where they could find a living master to write to, she answered, "I know one. His name is Harold Klemp."

So the children in this Swedish school began writing me letters with questions about God and dreams, and I wrote back. The teacher posted my responses on the cloakroom door, where the children could read them as they got their coats on to go outside and play at break. Yesterday the first letter had arrived. As the mother read the letter, she was able to connect the change in her child's attitude. She realized why her daughter, who had been despondent lately, suddenly seemed so happy.

The teacher learned that the way to serve ECK is to do the very best you can where you are, which she did with the children. She realized that she had been standing in her own way in her reluctance to talk about ECK. By working within the guidelines of the school to bring a little Light and Sound to the children, she had helped turn a sad child into a happy one.

51. Love Their Faults

A woman worked with a person who seemed to take great pleasure in insulting her. Some people in this world form friendships by making fun of their friends. It's a strange thing.

One day this woman went to a restaurant with her co-workers. The man began to insult the ECKist in a friendly way. She decided she couldn't take any more. Normally she's a quiet, soft-spoken person who hardly ever shows anger. But this time she flared up.

"If you couldn't insult me," she said to the man, "you wouldn't be able to think of one thing to say." The man was shocked. She got really angry and kept at him, talking louder and louder until people in the restaurant began looking around to see who was causing such a scene.

After the man and his wife had left, the ECKist stood with her husband and a friend out in the parking lot. "You were right to defend yourself," the friend said. "If he can dish it out, he better be able to take it."

"You're a saint to have been able to put up with him all these years," added the husband.

As they were talking, the woman's eyes kept going to a particular license plate on a nearby car. The license plate was enclosed in a frame and on the bottom of the frame were the words "Love their faults."

The friend continued, "Maybe this will teach him a lesson." And the license plate frame caught her eye again: Love their faults.

Finally it hit her. She started laughing. Her husband and the friend couldn't understand why she had suddenly gotten over her anger.

"Look at that license plate frame," she pointed. "The ECK is trying to tell us something."

The whole license plate frame read: Geologists love their faults. But she had read just the bottom part of the frame, Love their faults.

The woman knew it had been right to draw the line with this co-worker, but she felt she could've done it with love instead of anger. Because when we act with anger, we're acting from power. And when we act with love, we allow the other person to understand how we feel.

We let the other person know that he is not necessarily bad, but we do not want him to practice that sort of behavior in the future. Otherwise he will lose our friendship. It's very clean and very unemotional. It takes the anger out. It's spoken with love, the kind of love that is called charity in the Christian Bible.

52. Drumbeat of Time

A woman had been a member of ECKANKAR for almost two years. She was getting ready for her Second Initiation when she began to have a recurring experience in her spiritual exercises. First, she would hear the sound of a drum in the background, then she would find herself in a scene from another life.

The woman's husband was not in ECKANKAR, and although they loved each other, there had always been a kind of tension between them. Sometimes she felt very strong hatred for him, or fear. She didn't really understand it, because he was very kind to her.

One day during contemplation, the ECK Master Yaubl Sacabi took her to a ledge in space. In the background was the sound of a constant drumbeat. Yaubl Sacabi said to her, "This is where the time of the universe is kept." And she said, "But it sounds like the drumbeat on a Roman galley."

Immediately she found herself on one of those Roman ships. She was a tall strong man with reddish hair and beard and sunken eyes. She realized she was an oarsman pulling on a long oar in the hold of a huge ship.

The first thing that struck her was the musty smell from hundreds of people rowing and rowing in the cramped space. Then there was a feeling of cold, and she realized the ocean spray came in through the holes where the oars poked out. Other than the tiny amount of light that came through the holes, it was pitch dark. And it was a very miserable existence.

She realized she was very thirsty. An overseer was coming down the walkway. He treated the oarsmen like slaves. She was going to ask him for some water, but when she looked at him she felt a shock. There was a great wave of hate and anger in her, and she knew immediately this man was her husband in the present lifetime.

A few days later her husband noticed her reading an ECK discourse. He said, "Well, what are they trying to teach you now?"

"They're trying to teach me how not to hate you," she answered. And she understood how true this was.

This woman had had strong experiences long before she came to ECK. Experiences are not why she stays in ECK. She stays in ECK because of the understanding she's gaining of what her experiences mean.

So often people don't understand the relationships they have here. The relationships don't have to be based on such a strong experience as this woman's. She hadn't yet seen the times in the past when she was in the role of the overseer and her present husband was in the role of the slave. Life puts you on both ends so you can learn.

53. The Stalled Car

A husband was leaving for work one morning, and his car wouldn't start. It was cold, and his car had a teasing habit: the engine would turn over, but it didn't quite catch. He was used to grinding the starter motor a little bit more, saying, "Anytime now." Eventually the car would start, and he could drive off and get to work on time.

But this morning the car just wouldn't start. As he kept trying, the battery reserve got lower and lower. Pretty soon he was speaking very personally to the Mahanta, "Where are you when I need you? What is this ECK stuff? Just when a person needs it, it doesn't work." He threw in some colorful words.

About this same time, his wife's car was stalled in the middle of a busy street some distance away. He was at home in a nice, safe place, but she was stopped right in traffic. Unlike her husband, she got out of the car and started laughing, because she thought it was the funniest thing she'd ever seen.

Pretty soon another driver came by. "Can I help you push your car out of traffic?" he asked, and she agreed. When she was safely on the side of the road, the man said, "I know this great garage nearby. If you go there, they'll do a good job for you."

54. Forest Family

Our backyard feeder attracts a community of animals. Besides birds we have raccoons, squirrels, rabbits, chipmunks, and deer.

We call the rabbit Stretch. He is very cautious when he comes up to the feed dish, day or night. His only defense is his speed. Fear keeps him alive, and he's grown to be big and old.

Some say the rabbit is a symbol of fear and the deer is a symbol of gentleness. The other day a beautiful doe and a six-point buck came to the feed dishes. I heard a crash in the brush as they approached. The buck came up to the doe, bumped her out of the way, and stooped to the dish himself.

The rabbit sat opposite the dish, watching the buck. They were only four or five feet apart. I was proud of the rabbit's bravery. I told my wife, "The deer hasn't learned anything about gentleness, but the rabbit is learning something about bravery."

The rabbit and squirrels are about equal. Each waits for the other to eat first. If the rabbit's there first, the squirrels get a little pushy and boisterous, but they wait until the rabbit decides to leave the dish.

The most nervy of the creatures is a little chipmunk. He doesn't have any grace at all. When he comes out of the woods, he can hardly see over the top of the grass, but he runs straight at the squirrels. He zips through, coming up behind them, and he scares the living daylights out of them. The squirrels dash up the trees, and the chipmunk flies at the doves next. Pretty soon he's cleared the area and has the dish to himself.

The blue jays are outranked by the squirrels, but they're clever. They'll start making a lot of noise when the squirrels are at the dish. "Danger! Danger!" they scream. And the squirrels all run off into the trees, leaving the dish clear for the blue jays.

This little group makes up a spiritual community. They're learning their little lessons about when to come to the feed dish.

I look at them and think how much they are like people. People divide themselves in one way or another, by age, race, religion, or political affiliation. At the same time they forget we are all God's creatures. What really matters is how people treat each other in the human community.

55. Sugarbear

A teenage girl had a little dog named Sugarbear. Because the dog was such a wimp, everyone picked on it—other dogs, cats, even kittens.

After a while, Sugarbear began to develop some very strange behavior. For no apparent reason she would suddenly run out of the house right into the middle of the road. There she would do her little spray, right in the middle of the road, and just sit. Cars would stop, honk, and slowly drive around her. The teenager would try to call the dog in, but she wondered, Is Sugarbear losing her mind?

The teenager's friend came over one afternoon. As she was walking up to the house, she saw a cat spraying the bushes, marking its territory. Pretty soon a dog came by, sniffed at the bush and sprayed it. He had recaptured the territory for his own.

Finally a kitten came up, and it too marked the bush. Then, as the teenager's friend watched, Sugarbear came out of the house, looked around, and noticed the other animals. As if the dog knew that all the bushes had already been claimed by a sovereign power, Sugarbear ran into the middle of the road and sprayed. This was her territory. The poor little dog had to take what nobody else wanted.

People sometimes look at explorers who got on their little boats and sailed off to find a new land. The dangers were significant. Why did they do it? you might wonder. They were like little Sugarbear, going out in the middle of the road. They needed freedom, and they couldn't find it in the towns and in the settlements. They went where no one else had the courage to go.

56. Showing Charity

I was driving into the parking lot of a local discount store when I suddenly saw a white Cadillac tailing me. I wasn't paying too much attention until the person in the Cadillac began honking the horn over and over.

The driveway was huge, but the Cadillac cruised right on my left rear fender. The driver was upset. She thought I had cut in front of her while driving into the parking lot. She cruised on my bumper for a long time, then finally pulled around me, parked, and rushed into the store.

I don't like to be pushed, so when she came out of the store, I went over to her and said, "You probably didn't notice, but the freeway is over there." This was not the thing to say. She batted my ears down. When she left, I said, "That was really something." I could feel the waves of anger coming from her so strongly that I found myself shaking.

I wasn't afraid; I felt pretty calm inside. But sometimes when you're around a very angry person these energies that are being thrown out are so strong you can almost reach out and touch them.

I went to a pay phone and called my wife, just to balance out. "You won't believe what I just ran into," I said to her. The two-minute call was just enough.

But I kept running into people like this, especially at the post office. Our local post office has a tiny parking lot right off a busy street. Sometimes you can't drive into the parking lot right away, so you sit in the driveway or on the street. Then when you get into the parking lot, you often have to wait for a place.

One morning I was third in line, waiting for a place. I was halfway into the parking lot, but part of my car was in the street, so I was nervously looking over my right shoulder, watching for fast traffic.

The woman in the front of the line didn't see that there were two parking places available. Car number two finally got tired of waiting and drove into one of the spots. By now I figured the first car was waiting for someone inside the post office, so I took the second parking spot. Immediately she began honking at me.

She got out of her car and stalked over. I never realized a human being could scream so loud. She was taller than me, and stood over me, huffing. So I began apologizing.

"Excuse me," I said, "I didn't realize you weren't waiting for someone."

"It looked as if you were deliberately trying to edge me out," she said. "No, that wasn't the case at all," I said. So she calmed down a little bit.

So often when I am on the calm end of things and someone else loses his temper, I have a chance to either be angry in turn or show some charity. It's hard to show charity to someone who just flattened your ears, but this is how we give love to those in our family of life.

57. Sparky

An ECK couple had a dog who had a litter of twelve puppies. The smallest of the puppies was named Sparky. Sparky was a sickly pup right from the beginning; after six weeks the puppy still weighed only a pound.

The couple took the puppy to a vet. The doctor looked at Sparky and shook his head. "This little puppy isn't going to make it," he said. "He's going to go in a very short time."

One afternoon the husband came home early from work and found the puppy in his box in the bathroom. He saw that the puppy was about ready to translate, so the man went into contemplation.

He sat down, shut his eyes, and put his attention on the Spiritual Eye, which is in the center of the forehead. He began to chant HU, an ancient name for God. As he chanted HU, the Inner Master came to him.

"It looks like Sparky's going to translate," the man said to the Inner Master. "I want to help. What can we do?"

"We actually do very little," said the Mahanta. "We let the Holy Spirit do it."

This was a surprise to the man and a spiritual lesson. Too often we find in the prayers of people that they are trying to tell God what to do. They pull on God's robe, "Excuse me, you've overlooked something important." Their health isn't what they'd like it to be, or they're having problems with their spouse.

People who pray like that are talking to themselves in a closed room, without echoes. Their faith needs constant proof. They create their own God, with the qualities that they think God should have.

God takes care of all matters with greater wisdom than we can ever know—from the smallest puppy's translation to any other highly spiritual matter.

Contemplations . . .

You can't make yourself closer to God by hating someone else, whether you believe it's righteous anger or not. The relationship between Soul—which is you—and God is one of love. And where there's pure love, there is no room for anger of any kind.

* * *

People learn by hardship. People learn by facing themselves. And often when people face themselves, they point the finger at others. They see all their faults in their neighbors. But it's really a test by the negative power against them. After we fail the same tests a hundred times, even the most thick-headed Soul learns.

* * *

The ECK works in subtle ways, but you have to remember to ask. Most people can't hear. Even in ECK, you learn how to listen and how to see these messages from the Holy Spirit that come to you and everyone every day.

* * *

When people interfere with each other, they are not expressing divine love. How many people today do this constantly? Even we in ECK don't always realize that when we violate the Law of Noninterference, we are doing so because of a lack of love.

* * *

If we realize that our field of dreams is not the same as someone else's field of dreams, we'll get along better with that person. This is a hard thing to learn sometimes.

* * *

We, as ECKists, are required spiritually to act with the greatest degree of responsibility both to ourselves and to others. This is what it means to be part of the community of ECK, to be part of the cosmic system of life.

The Mahanta gave this ECK initiate and her husband protection, first through the waking dream of the smoke alarm that sounded a low-battery warning, then through the Golden-tongued Wisdom of a friend bringing a verbal warning.

Chapter Six

Divine Protection

58. Smoke Alarm

One night a woman was asleep in bed when her smoke alarm made a loud peeping sound. It was warning that the battery was getting low and needed to be replaced. The woman really didn't want to change the battery in the middle of the night, so she disconnected the smoke alarm and went back to sleep.

Before she fell back to sleep, she promised herself that she would install a new battery in the morning, but when morning came she had forgotten.

Later that day, a friend called. This friend had the ability to see things in other people's lives that were prophetic. Her friend was very distraught.

"I'm so worried about you," she said. "I see you as a small white cloud. This black cloud is hovering next to you, and it's almost engulfing you." The friend was afraid the woman wouldn't believe her warning; in the past when she had told people of coming danger, they had just dismissed it.

The ECKist tried to figure out her friend's warning. I wonder if it's spiritual or physical, she thought.

When she got home that evening, she met her husband as he was coming into the kitchen. She switched on a fluorescent light, and there was a big flash. The bulb had burned out; there was smoke all over the kitchen. By now the ECKist was concerned. This was the third unusual thing that had happened to her in twenty-four hours. The incident reminded her to replace the battery in the smoke alarm.

The next day the ECKist went out and bought another fluorescent bulb. As she was going into the kitchen to replace it, she flipped the light switch. Again there was a loud flash and smoke came out of the light fixture. So she shut off the switch, went to the fuse box, and turned off all electricity to the kitchen.

When her husband came home, she told him about the series of events. "I think the ECK is trying to tell us something," she said. So he got a stepladder to look at the light fixture. As he was taking it apart, he found that the entire fixture was burned black. The fixture had shorted out entirely. The couple had narrowly averted a house fire. If the woman had left the switch in the kitchen on, the fixture would probably have caught fire.

Here's an occasion where the Mahanta gave this ECK initiate and her husband protection, first through the waking dream of the smoke alarm that sounded a low-battery warning, then through the Golden-tongued Wisdom of a friend bringing a verbal warning. Finally protection was given through the waking dream of the kitchen light that burned out.

When protection comes, several different elements are often working at the same time. Most likely you have been given one, two, or three warnings already. The couple received three separate warnings, and the woman was able to listen.

The *ECK Dream Discourses* and the Spiritual Exercises of ECK help you develop your spiritual awareness so that you can understand that life is a series of interconnected wheels. Very little can happen to you without it being known ahead of time by you. All you have to do is learn to be aware.

59. School Party

An ECK couple had three children, two boys of six and four years old and a girl of one-and-a-half. At the end of the school year, their rural school had planned a party for the children.

The mother in the family went to the school early the day of the party, telling her children to stay home for a short while. Someone would come by to pick them up for the party.

But the children were so eager to go that the six-year-old boy dressed all the children. Then they locked the door and set off for the school.

The only problem was that they didn't know where the school was. A school bus took them to school every day, and none of the children knew the way.

The older boy decided they should walk along the road the school bus followed until they came to the highway. When they reached it, the children didn't know which way to go. The older boy led them along the edge of the busy highway. Cars were speeding by them, but the children hugged the edge of the road and remained unhurt.

A former neighbor of the family happened to be driving past when he saw the children. Although he thought he recognized the oldest boy, he wondered whether to stop—a dangerous maneuver in such high-speed traffic. But he pulled off the road and got out of the car.

"What are you doing here?" he asked them. The older boy explained that they were on the way to their school party. Knowing they would likely be killed trying to cross the highway, the neighbor decided to drive them to the school.

When the mother saw her children and heard what danger they had been in, she became very tearful. But she knew the ECK had wrapped Its cloak of protection around her three children as they walked along the busy highway.

60. Nail in the Passageway

A father in Africa had a teenage son. When the boy was fifteen years old, he stepped on something, got tetanus, and died.

The father was an ECKist and wanted to meet his son on the inner planes. So he went into contemplation and chanted HU. And during contemplation, he went in the Soul body and met his son through Soul Travel. First they greeted each other; it was a time of love and joy.

Then the father asked his son, "How did you hurt yourself? Where did you step on something that gave you tetanus?"

The son said, "In the corner of the passageway that leads to the kitchen is a nail. That is what I stepped on."

When the father returned from contemplation, he got up from his bed and went into the passageway. In the corner near the kitchen, he found a rusty nail sticking out of the floor. It was out of the way, but his son had just happened to step on it.

The father was able to pull the nail out of the floorboard and make sure that no one else's health would be endangered. Even though he went through the anguish of his son's translation, through this experience he was able to find that his son lived on. Life continues; it is a steady stream of consciousness. Through the love bond between them, the son had been able to offer protection to the family in a time of need.

If there is a strong love bond between you, you can meet with relatives that have passed on. But eventually you give that up. We don't spend this life with our head in the clouds, hoping and living for the moment of translation. Life is life. Each plane has something to teach. The world to live in is the world of today, here on the physical plane.

61. Bank Robbery

A woman had to run some errands one afternoon and especially wanted to make it to the bank before it closed. But she got caught up in reading *Unlocking the Puzzle Box*, feeling grateful for all the blessings that had come into her life, and she was a bit late leaving.

The bank was just around the corner. She got into her car and rushed down there, hoping she wasn't too late.

When she got there she saw that the bank doors were locked. Inside the bank were police and a few customers. A bank robbery had just occurred.

If she had gone when she had originally planned to, she would have been caught in the building right in the middle of a bank robbery. That was an experience she really didn't need. So at just the right moment, something in the ECK book had caught and held her attention. It caused her to read a little bit longer than she had planned.

The Holy Spirit had stepped in and given her the protection she needed at that moment.

62. Fire in the Kitchen

A man who lived in Africa came home from work one day to make himself a quick lunch. As he lit the two-burner kerosene stove, he remembered that his wife had been complaining about it leaking. But he was in a hurry.

He bent down to get a knife. As he stood up, he saw that the entire stove and the top of the table the stove sat on was engulfed in flames. He grabbed an aluminum washbasin and put it over the stove, trying to snuff out the fire. It didn't work. He tried to snuff out the flames with other utensils, but the flames just kept spreading.

Suddenly he had a strong feeling to chant the word *HU*. As this came into his mind, he began to chant in a very low, strong voice and slowly held his hand over the fire.

To us in Western countries, this would seem foolhardy. "Watch out, you'll burn your hand!" we'd say. But this was his home. And he had this strong understanding of what he should do. Later, he said he had felt like Moses parting the Red Sea, putting his hand over a thing to make it work right.

As he held his hand over the flames, he heard a clicking sound, as if the grip of some invisible being had let go of the fire. All of a sudden, the fire extinguished itself. It just went away.

The entire tabletop had been burned, and the

stove was destroyed; but at least the man had saved his home. He also had learned something very important: by chanting HU, the love song to God, help had come to him in a very unexpected way just when he needed it.

63. The Power of HU

In 1981 a man living in Ghana was strolling down the street, enjoying the afternoon, when suddenly a soldier came up to him with a dagger and accused him of something he knew nothing about.

Ghana at that time was a country in political turmoil and under military rule. The soldier forced the man into a shack to interrogate him. "Unless you confess," the soldier threatened, "I'm going to harm you."

The man surrendered completely to God. If this is my time to go, he thought, then I'll go.

Just as the soldier was about to begin beating the man, the man's Spiritual Eye opened. He very clearly saw the letters *H-U,* then he heard the sound of HU. This was years before he had ever heard of ECKANKAR.

At exactly the same moment, the soldier said gruffly, "If you're not guilty, then get out of here."

When the man learned of ECKANKAR a few years later, a piece of the puzzle fell into place. He realized that HU, this name of God, had a power unlike any other.

The power of HU can benefit everyone, whether they are Muslim or Christian or of any other belief. It doesn't change one's religion, but it will enhance it.

64. Unusual Protection

A businessman went to work early in the morning one day. About 10:00 a.m. he had a surprise visit from his wife. She was carrying their oldest child.

"What happened?" he asked, alarmed.

His wife said that after he had left for work the girl had been playing outside when an electrical wire fell on her. Because the electricity was still flowing through the wire, no one dared touch the girl to help her. The live wire lay on her for ten minutes.

When someone finally arrived to turn off the electricity, the daughter got up and ran to her mother. The mother decided to bring the girl to her father. "Let's get her to the hospital," the father said.

So the family went to the hospital.

The doctors were amazed. "This is the strangest thing we've ever seen," they said. "How can this child still be alive?" They wondered over it but pronounced her in good health, so the mother took her daughter back home.

Later the mother and father were discussing the situation and decided that unusual protection had been granted them from the Mahanta. This is one example of how the Mahanta is a friend to you.

65. Malaria Pills

A group of ECKists were traveling with me to the ECK African Seminar in Nigeria. As a precaution, we all had to take malaria pills. Nobody wanted to, but it was important. We took a pill a week before we got there, the day we got there, and then once each week for four weeks.

The night before we left for Africa, our group was staying together in a hotel in the Netherlands. We were there for the ECK European Seminar. A few of us went out to eat, and I asked the others, "By the way, did you take your malaria pill?" Everyone had except one man who said he had forgotten. "Don't worry," he told the group, "If you remind me, I'll do it when I get back to the room." But when we went back to the hotel, we all forgot.

In the middle of the night, I woke up. "We forgot to tell him to take his malaria pill," I said to my wife. "We can tell him in the morning," she said, and we settled back down to sleep. Then I remembered something else. "He has to take the pill with food," I said. "We'll tell him in the morning," my wife said again.

The next morning we met the man for breakfast. He looked at me strangely. "About 5:00 a.m. I woke up suddenly and clearly heard you say, 'You have to take your malaria pill,'" he said. "So I got out of bed and got the pill. I was just crawling back under the covers for a little more sleep when I heard your voice say, 'But you've got to take it with food.' So I ate some cookies."

"Wouldn't it be funny," he added, "if as you're telling this story during your seminar talk today, all the people in the audience who are going to Africa stood up and said, 'So that's why I got up at 5:00 a.m. and took my malaria pill.'"

We joked about it some more, but the truth is that the Inner Master works this way many times. Protection is given to those who listen inwardly.

Contemplations . . .

We don't spend this life with our head in the clouds, hoping and living for the moment of translation. Life is life. Each plane has something to teach. The world to live in is the world of today, here on the physical plane.

* * *

Life is a series of interconnected wheels. Very little can happen to you without it being known ahead of time by you. All you have to do is learn to be aware.

* * *

Often when protection comes into your life, it has several different elements working at the same time. When these things come into your life, most likely you have been given one, two, or three warnings already.

* * *

The power of HU can benefit everyone, whether they are Muslim or Christian or of any other belief. It doesn't change one's religion, but it will enhance it.

The woman realized that she was very much like Peanut when she had first come into ECKANKAR. The Mahanta had taken her out of her cage, her own little world, and said, "Here, you're free. You can run around in this bigger room."

Chapter Seven

Spiritual Tests and Spiritual Growth

66. Peanut's Hard Road to Freedom

A woman was offered a rabbit as a gift from a friend. The rabbit was one-and-a-half years old and had light brown fur. The woman took it home and put it in a little cage and decided to call it Peanut.

On the first day, the woman took off the top of the cage, thinking the rabbit might like to explore his new home. But the rabbit wouldn't leave the cage. On the second day she walked by the rabbit's cage and saw it crouching there.

She lifted Peanut out of his cage that afternoon and took him to her bedroom. Peanut hopped around carefully, testing his new freedom. It was the first time he had been out of his cage on his own. All of a sudden he ran really fast around the room, then jumped straight up in the air, expressing his joy at this freedom.

She was so happy for him. But after a few days watching the rabbit roam around, she realized she wasn't getting any work done. So she decided to take him back to the kitchen. She expected that he would jump out of his cage and begin exploring, as he had in the bedroom. But Peanut crouched in his cage all day. He wouldn't move.

The woman tried everything to encourage the rabbit. She brought over a little rug and set Peanut on it. He immediately hopped back into the cage.

She tried again, he went back into the cage.

For about a week, the most Peanut would do was stick his nose over the edge of the cage and sniff the air. One day he took a little hop onto the rug, then hopped right back into the cage. He hopped back and forth several times that week. Finally he began staying out of the cage for longer periods.

"This isn't going very well," the woman said to her friend. "I'm going to try coaxing Peanut out of the room. I'd like him to have the run of the whole house." So she lay down in the doorway and talked softly to the scared rabbit, "Come on, Peanut! You can do it! Be brave!"

On the third day the rabbit finally gathered his courage and hopped into the hallway. As if frightened by his own daring, he dashed back and forth a few times, then hurried back to the kitchen. But pretty soon he was making forays into a third room. His ears pricked up, his body relaxed, and he looked like he felt really good.

There's nothing quite as afraid as a rabbit because it has no natural defense except speed. The woman realized that she was very much like Peanut when she had first come into ECKANKAR. The Mahanta had taken her out of her cage, her own little world, and said, "Here, you're free. You can run around in this bigger room." But she was too scared. She didn't want to step out of her comfortable little world.

Gradually as the Mahanta tried to take her to new spiritual levels and show her there was nothing to fear, she was able to relax. She was able to accept and enjoy the greater spiritual freedom she found in ECKANKAR.

67. Could I Please Pay for That Honey?

A mother went shopping with her bratty daughter. They were standing in the checkout line, waiting to pay for groceries. The mother had a shopping cart filled with food, and the little girl had her hands all over it. She kept pushing the cart against the back of the woman ahead of them in line. "Bam, bam, bam," she said, as she rammed the cart into the woman.

Finally the woman turned around. "Could you please ask your daughter to stop? That hurts!" she said to the mother.

"I will not," the mother answered. "My daughter is being raised the antiauthoritarian way. And I wish her to have freedom." And the little girl went right on banging this woman in the back.

About this time, a customer standing right behind the mother and little girl began opening a jar of honey. Everyone in line watched as he removed the lid and slowly walked over to the little girl. Very carefully he poured the contents of the jar of honey on top of the little girl's head.

The jar of honey was half empty before the mother could speak. "What are you doing?" she screamed. "Stop! Stop doing that to my little girl!"

"Don't stop me," replied the young man. "I was raised the antiauthoritarian way."

As the last few drops were falling on the little

girl's head, someone in the back of the line called out, "Could I please pay for that honey?"

Often we can get a lot of our own lessons by watching the experiences of others. When a person gets an experience because of a lack of self-discipline, we are usually very quick to pick it up. "He doesn't have any self-discipline," we say. "That's why he's a failure in business." All the things we do in the physical life are little lessons for us to learn spiritually, so that someday we can become a Co-worker with God.

A Co-worker with God is someone who has learned self-discipline in spiritual things.

68. Busy Signal

Recently I stretched my computer skills. I began tapping into a computer information service to get access to an on-line encyclopedia. I like to use it in my research for writing the ECK discourses and books.

But I learned fast that before you even get close to accessing information from these computer services, you have to learn how to work with the software and equipment. First you learn about modems. Then you learn how little you actually know about modems.

One night I sat in front of my computer, trying to dial the on-line service. Ideally, the modem dials the number, the computer goes through a code-word check, then you get linked up. But it wasn't working. I went around and around, always getting the same message on my screen: "Busy signal. Try again later."

After quite a few tries, I finally noticed the problem: The phone line wasn't plugged in. The computer had been talking to itself. The message had been unable to get out of my house because I didn't have a telephone line plugged into the computer.

In situations like this, you're usually waiting, all geared up and ready to go. You've got a plan of action: you're going to get into the database. But when you forget to make the spiritual connection, or plug the phone line into the wall, you get yourself worked up for nothing. You end up wasting a lot of effort.

69. Video Quarter

As I was leaving a video arcade, a teenage girl of about fifteen or sixteen came away from a group of her friends and asked me for a quarter so she could call home. I knew she had used her last quarter on the games, the quarter she was supposed to save in case she had to call her parents for a ride.

But she was embarrassed and wasn't very good at public begging. "What's it for?" I said. "I just want to call home," she said. "Or another video game?" I asked her. I have a teenage daughter, and I know how that works.

"No, really, it's to call home," she insisted.

"OK," I said, "here's a quarter." But as she started to leave, I added, "One thing more."

"If you ever feel that it's important to pay back this quarter, give it to one of the smaller kids here. But give it to them so that they don't feel as if they owe it to you," I said.

She stood there, and she had the most puzzled look on her face. It was a beautiful thing to see. I was leaving her with this problem in the shape of one little quarter. I knew that was a pretty heavy load to put on a teenager, but I thought she could handle it. I was telling her that there's a responsibility to give back a gift to life, and when you give the gift back, it has to be with no strings attached.

Kids come up to me in video arcades all the time, asking for things. Usually I don't give anything to them because it teaches them the wrong thing. You cannot develop spiritual knowledge and wisdom by living off other people without having paid into the system at some time.

But if this teenager was really as sharp as I think she was, she'll give the quarter to the next little kid who asks her. And she'll tell him, "If you ever feel it's important to return this quarter to somebody else, give it to them. But don't make them feel as if they owe you."

70. The Man Who Met Paul Twitchell

A man met Paul Twitchell in an Ocean Beach, California, coffee shop. They were both regulars in this place, and Paul would talk with him each morning about the teachings of ECK. The man couldn't understand a word Paul was saying because Paul was using religious concepts the man had never come across before.

One day Paul began his usual conversation with the man but then he stopped in midsentence. "You're just not ready for ECKANKAR," Paul said, looking at the man sitting next to him. "Go out into the world and look for whatever it is you are looking for. Maybe someday you'll find it." That was the last time they saw each other.

A few minutes after Paul left the coffee shop that day, a feeling of ecstasy came over the man. He had never felt like this before in his life. Everything was sparkling clear, and he was in a state of euphoria.

For many years after, the man searched for something that would bring this state of euphoria back. It took almost twenty years before he found ECKANKAR again and realized that this euphoria was feeling the love of God.

There are people who are critical of Paul. He was up to shenanigans in one way or another for most of his life. But once he found his mission with ECKANKAR, it became his breath and life force, day and night. He lived and spoke it constantly.

When people were receptive to what Paul offered and understood what he was saying, they got the gift of love. But often those people who didn't understand, like the man in the coffee shop, also got the gift of love.

71. Shredded Wheat

One winter day I ran out of birdseed. I said to my wife, "I forgot to go to the store. I don't know what to feed them until it opens tomorrow." My wife said, "You can give them some of my shredded wheat." My wife just loved her shredded wheat; it was her special cereal that she ate every morning. She'd been eating it a lot lately.

So I took the box, poured two dishes full, then carried them outside for the birds and animals.

In a few hours we looked out the window to check. There were tracks in the snow that led up to each dish, but nobody had touched the shredded wheat.

The next morning we looked again. There were a lot more tracks, but the shredded wheat was still there. So I went to the store and bought some birdseed, and threw away the two bowls of shredded wheat.

After that my wife didn't eat her special shredded wheat so much. She figured that if the birds and animals wouldn't touch it, maybe there wasn't any value in it.

Sometimes you can learn from nature. Sometimes the lessons you learn are very good ones, but they catch you by surprise. Some very wise beings in the neighborhood put their stamp on my wife's shredded wheat. And it wasn't the stamp of approval.

72. Just One Step Away

A woman worked in a medical office where the doctor was unkind to her. She was always being scolded for this or that. She finally couldn't stand it, so she quit; she felt that no matter how bad it was out there in the world, she'd be better off without a job than working for that doctor.

Right after she quit, the woman had an accident where she broke her jaw. She lay at home recuperating, wondering what she should do as the bills began piling up.

One morning she got a call from another doctor in the same medical building where she had worked before. He asked her if she would work on a temporary basis in his office while one of his regular employees was on maternity leave. She said yes and started work the next week.

The woman loved her new job. In comparison, this office was like heaven. One day she noticed that the voices on the other side of this wall of her new office sounded very much like the people who had worked in the unkind doctor's office. She realized the offices were back to back.

All this time she had been a few footsteps away from heaven. But she had to go through a lot of trial and tribulation to land on the other side of the wall.

Sometimes it's like this in your spiritual life.

When things are hard for you, you wonder, What's happening? Have you forgotten me, God?

But sometimes you need the experience of leaving the old place first, of having the will to say, "This is not the way I want to live my life." There are a lot of little things that go along with a decision like this. When you go from one state of consciousness to another, there are always adjustments to be made.

73. Shopping Mall

A man went with his wife and friend to a shopping mall. As they were strolling down the main area of the mall, looking into the shops on either side, the man began to discourse on the similarity between the stream of people going into the shops and the journey of Soul through the lower worlds.

"Notice all the people walking down the corridor in a stream," he said. "Every so often a person will leave the mainstream as their attention draws them into a particular shop. But the crowd keeps moving."

The man went on to say how this was very much like life. "Humanity is moving through life," he explained. "As humanity we have moved through past lives together. We each have gone off into our little shops: sometimes we were weavers, sometimes sailors, sometimes artists.

"Each of these professions is like a shop in a shopping mall. It's the place where our interests and attention drew us. We spend a certain amount of time in each shop, like a lifetime spent learning things, completely absorbed in the spiritual moment. Except that we were doing it unconsciously."

The wife and friend looked properly impressed by this high-minded discourse. The man went on to explain that once someone gains a measure of spirituality, he becomes aware of his visits to the shops. He begins to be able to resist the pull and live more consciously.

As he was explaining this idea, his wife suddenly disappeared into a dress shop. Smiling, the man turned to his friend. "See?" he said. "She's lost in her little world. Lost in her shop."

"I see what you mean," said his friend.

The man went on to explain something else as they neared a camera shop. While he was absorbed in his sentence, his friend stopped to look in the window, admiring different lenses. Then he wandered into the shop, totally captivated.

They are lost in their own little worlds, the speaker thought to himself. Feeling very smug, he continued down the mall. Suddenly he passed a hardware store. Without another thought, he was inside, looking at drills and saws and all kinds of attachments.

Minutes later, or maybe it was hours later, he felt a tap on his shoulder. It was his wife. "Are you lost?" she grinned at him. "I guess so," the man said sheepishly.

It's fine to stop in little shops that attract you in life, but the point is to do it consciously. Know that you have left the crowd for a moment to stop somewhere you want to. And when you have had your fill of that shop, leave it and consciously rejoin the group of people moving in the corridor of life. In other words, move at will, consciously.

74. Learning to Back Up

Molly, our little dog, was quite old. She had lost her sight and hearing over the last few years of her life. In her old age, she was filled with love but she was also just as stubborn as ever.

Before she died, she got it in mind to understand the great unmovable. It happened to be our library bookcase. She would get up from her bed, come over to the bookcase, and try to push it over. She'd put her head against the bookcase and push until she'd practically stand on her head. Then she'd fall over on her side.

Molly would get to her feet and turn around in tight little circles, trying to get her bearings. Figuring the bookcase was the only thing in her way, she'd put her head against it, trying to move it with her little body. Funny thing was, Molly never thought to back up and go around. That would have been the easiest way to get out of her predicament.

Most of our problems are caused because we spiritually cannot back up. We come up against something bigger than we are. We say, "I'm going to beat this." Or, "I haven't tried hard enough." This usually goes against the flow of ECK.

Whenever you come up against whatever is the great unmovable for you, the simplest way to get around it is to sing HU. If you can remember, stand back and sing HU. Then wait to see what comes through. The ECK will give you some insight on how to approach your bookcase—your problem—from another angle.

75. A Special Name

A Higher Initiate in ECK was very well known among chelas. He gave a lot of talks at seminars and people would stop him in the halls as he walked by.

At one seminar a chela came up to him and started telling him how much she had admired his talks. She'd admired them for years. As she went on and on, the Higher Initiate grew a little embarrassed.

"Thank you very much," he said, but the chela had more.

"I wanted to tell you personally that I admire your talks so much that I am going to name my mule after you," finished the chela. She beamed at the Higher Initiate.

The Higher Initiate thanked her again and walked off, chuckling to himself. The ECK always finds a way to keep us humble, he thought.

76. Scorched Iron

We had arrived at our hotel for an ECKANKAR seminar and were unpacking in our rooms. I wanted to iron some of my clothes that had gotten wrinkled, so I called the front desk to borrow an iron.

When the iron and ironing board arrived, I noticed that the bottom of the iron was very scorched. It was covered with a gumlike material. We called the desk again and asked for another iron, but the second one they brought us was scorched as well. Then I called a friend who was staying in the next room who had also ordered an iron. Not only was his iron scorched, but the ironing board they sent wouldn't stand up; it had a missing leg.

I wondered about this all day. Why had we all gotten scorched irons, plus an ironing board that was missing a leg?

When I was going over notes for my talk that evening, I realized that the ECK was telling me something.

When you use an iron that's scorched, instead of making your clothes beautiful, it burns them or leaves residue on them. Instead of making something better, you cause more problems if you use an iron that has problems.

People come to the path of ECK like scorched irons. They bring all these karmic problems with them. Before the iron can work the way it's intended to, it's got to go through a scrubbing. Someone's got to take steel wool to it and get the gum off.

People who try to fix themselves spiritually or try to solve a problem they see with the human consciousness rely on their own means instead of relying on the Mahanta. Their attempts will actually burn more clothes.

77. Winning the Raffle

A Higher Initiate had always put himself at the cutting edge of life. He loved to try new things. When he was first in ECK, he couldn't always tell if his ideas followed the way the Holy Spirit works. But this didn't stop him from doing things for ECK.

For a while people would come mopping up after him. They covered for him until he learned what ECK was all about and how the Holy Spirit worked so he could express himself properly.

Ten years passed, and the ECKist learned to explain ECK very well. He learned how to tell people about the Sound and Light, and about HU. He sang HU in his own life all the time.

One summer the Higher Initiate learned that the local symphony orchestra was having a raffle. The first prize was a BMW.

The man thought to himself, I could use a nice car. He wondered if he could bend the principles of ECK a little to help him get the car. But in ECK we don't use visualization techniques to achieve material gain. We sing HU to open ourselves as a channel for the Holy Spirit.

Before ECK, the Higher Initiate had learned about thinking and growing rich. He wanted that car, so he visualized it. He got a dummy key, and he held it and looked at it every day. Once a month for three months he went to a dealer and test-drove a BMW. He said to his friends, "I'm going to make that BMW part of my world. I'll think and dream about it so much that I can't help but win that car."

The Higher Initiate got a call from the symphony one morning: He had won the raffle.

But he hadn't won the first prize, the BMW. He won second prize: two plane tickets to Paris.

Coincidentally, ECKANKAR was having the ECK European Seminar in Paris that summer. So the ECKist got to attend.

He was very happy about the raffle, even though he didn't win the car of his dreams. The ECK had worked it out differently.

The point of this story is that whatever you hope to gain in life is going to take some effort on your part. The greater the goal that you're looking to achieve, the more you're going to have to work to get it.

All through this Higher Initiate's life, he had given to the ECK. All he could do was give and give, without thinking of reward. He put forth the effort to win the raffle, but the Holy Spirit always decides what's best for a person. What did he need for his spiritual unfoldment? Apparently, the Higher Initiate needed to go to Paris.

78. The Old Red Bicycle

On the inner planes, I was walking by the ocean. Ahead of me walked two teenagers. They parted at the waterfront, and one of them got on an old red Schwinn bicycle.

The boy had evidently had the bike since he was very young. Somewhere along the line he had gotten tired of the color red, so he had tried to paint the bike with white house paint. He was embarrassed by the results, so he drew psychedelic swirls and whirls all over the frame. It was a real eyesore.

The boy began pedaling his bike up a steep hill, and I walked behind him. Because the hill was so steep, I was able to stay right behind him. I caught up at the top of the hill.

"Nice bike," I commented. Underneath the paint was a sturdy bike.

"It's for sale," the boy said. I like to encourage people, so I said, "I'll give you twenty dollars for it," about fifteen more than he was going to get for it anywhere else.

"OK," he said. "Come over to my place. My folks are home, and we can talk there."

So I went over to his house, came into his living room, and sat down while he went to talk to his mother. He told her he had found someone to buy his bike for twenty dollars, but evidently she wanted him to be a tougher negotiator.

When he came back into the room, I held out the twenty dollars. But he walked over to the bike and began to take off the basket and the light.

"What are you doing?" I asked.

"They're extra," he said. "You want them, you pay extra."

"No," I said, "our deal was twenty dollars for the bike as it stands there." He kept taking off the light.

"No deal," I said. Then he said, "What?" "We had a deal," I said. "Twenty dollars is more than you're going to get for this bike anywhere else. I was trying to do you a favor. Now you try to wrangle me for a few more dollars for this stuff you're stripping off. No deal."

Then his mother came running out. "Just put everything back on," she said, trying to smooth things over. "You can have the bike for twenty."

But I said, "I don't want it. I don't need the bike. It would have made my day easier, because I have a long way to walk today. But I don't mind walking. And I don't need material things. All I wanted to do was pass the time in conversation and encourage you to do something with a bike you no longer have any use for. I would have found a way to give the bicycle to someone else."

The young man tried to open up the deal again. But I shook my head. "You gave your word, then you broke it. You can't do that," I told him. "We had a deal, and we were both keeping it in good faith until you tried to renege. That's where you went wrong. You and I had an understanding."

The boy came after me, pleading. I felt for him, and I wanted to turn around and give him the money. But I realized that it wouldn't help him spiritually. He wouldn't learn the lesson.

I was trying to teach the boy about spiritual freedom. The lesson was, Keep your word. Be strong if you feel something is right. Unless you are strong, you won't be able to go forward and accept the love that the ECK, the Holy Spirit, is offering. The weak cannot stand the love of God.

79. Copper Coins

A woman was nearing retirement in a company she had been with for many years. She had about a year left but wondered if she should work extra years to put more money aside.

One day in contemplation she said to the ECK, "Please give me a sign about my retirement. Three weeks before I am supposed to retire, show me a little copper coin with a hole near the edge." A coin like that was not very common, she reasoned. She really didn't expect to see this sign from the ECK for another eleven months.

A week later she saw an unusual pair of earrings made of two copper coins. Each earring had a hole punched in one end, just like her sign. The woman laughed to herself at the coincidence, thinking earrings didn't count. So she tried to put it out of her mind.

In just two weeks the company unexpectedly offered certain employees a cash bonus for early retirement. She was one of them. The ECK had given her the sign she'd asked for precisely three weeks before.

She had asked for this insight or confirmation because she felt she really wasn't too good at making decisions. The proof sent by the ECK caught her off guard. But these little things happen constantly. ECKists who realize how the Holy Spirit works in everyday life look for these things.

The miracles that happened in the early Christian church still happen today. To see and benefit from them, all we need to do is open our consciousness through the Spiritual Exercises of ECK.

80. Garage Door Opener

One morning I saw a daddy longlegs in the bathroom under the shelf, so I decided to take him outside. I got a glass and gently scooped him into it with an index card, then carried him to the garage to set him in the yard.

Carefully balancing the glass with one hand, I pushed the button for the garage door opener. The door opened slowly, then there was an enormous blue flash. The light had burned out.

It startled me so much that I almost dropped the glass. The spider fell onto the garage floor and scurried away.

"As long as I'm here, I'll replace that burned-out light bulb," I said to my wife. So I went back inside to get a new bulb.

I came back out, stood on a stepladder, and screwed in the new bulb. It stayed lit for about five seconds, then went out. "Oh, no," I said, "we've got big problems." It looked like there was a short in the garage door opener.

"Now the door's going to be frozen in the open position and anyone can come in and steal my lawnmower or snow thrower," I told my wife. Maybe this isn't so bad, I thought.

After thinking about this problem and how I was going to fix it, it occurred to me to try the garage door opener again. A little skeptical, I walked over to the button and pressed it. To my surprise, the light came on immediately and the door closed.

I realized our garage door opener has a ten-minute timer. The light comes on when the door opens, then it shuts off after ten minutes. Apparently by the time I went inside and found a new bulb, nine minutes and fifty-five seconds had passed.

Sometimes forces of illusion try to make us see things through a cloud. We draw the wrong conclusions like I did when I thought the garage door opener was broken. But because I listened to the inner nudge to try once more, the illusion was broken instead.

81. Two Gardeners and Twelve Trees

Early one morning I was looking out my hotel window and saw two gardeners. Each had a shovel. They were standing near a row of twelve trees which had been planted alongside the road.

The gardeners took their shovels and dug and dug. They yanked on the first tree in the row, tugging it back and forth to pull it from the ground. At first I thought the tree was crooked and they were just trying to straighten it. But soon they had it out of the ground.

Then they went to the second tree. Through much sweat and toil, the gardeners dug the second tree out of the ground. It must have taken them twenty minutes. I didn't know why it would be so hard, or why they didn't use a machine.

The gardeners continued to work down the row of trees. When they couldn't get a tree out of the ground by digging or pulling it back and forth, they sat down and made plans how to attack the little tree from a different angle.

I watched them for a while then went to lunch. When I came back I saw that ten of the trees were down. One tree was full of greenery, so they had left it. From my viewpoint far away, the last tree looked very dead to me, but it must have had one little green leaf on it, because they left it too.

"More than likely," I said to my wife, "these trees were planted last season. It must have been a hard year of drought. They put in twelve, and they got two good trees that will last."

So often people who come to the spiritual path, looking for truth, stay for a season. Perhaps there is a drought. Maybe ten of the twelve don't get the water they need. But two do, showing that it was possible for some to thrive in that area.

The task which faces the Mahanta, the Living ECK Master is very similar to the job of a gardener. All the people who come to the Mahanta, the Living ECK Master want a chance to grow and bloom. But for some, the climate's too hot, there's too much sun, or they dry out.

These people come to ECK and leave after one season. They haven't found what they want, so they go to some other climate to thrive. The Living ECK Master comes along and says, "Well, ten didn't work. Two may work. We'll give them extraspecial care: a little extra love, more water, fertilizer, and whatever it takes to make a tree grow right." Because they hung on.

Contemplations . . .

The tests that are easy for us are difficult for others. This is the nature of life. And it means that we, as human beings, must learn patience and compassion. The wheel always turns.

*   *   *

When you go from one state of consciousness to another, there are always adjustments to be made. Sometimes you need the experience of leaving the old place first, of having the will to say, "This is not the way I want to live my life." There are a lot of little things that go along with a decision like this.

*   *   *

The miracles that happened in the early Christian church still happen today. To see and benefit from them, all we need to do is open our consciousness through the Spiritual Exercises of ECK.

*   *   *

All the things we do in the physical life are little lessons for us to learn spiritually, so that someday we become a Co-worker with God.

*   *   *

A Co-worker with God is someone who has learned self-discipline in spiritual things.

The Mahanta said, "The golden cup is Soul. The more the ECK flows in and out of the cup, the more Soul shines of Its own golden light."

Chapter Eight

Spiritual Exercises of ECK

82. The Golden Cup

An ECK chela wanted to remember his dreams so he created this spiritual exercise.

As he goes to bed, he visualizes a golden goblet on his nightstand. He says to himself, When I go to sleep and have my dream experiences, the ECK is going to fill this cup with the Light and Sound of God. He tells himself that each dream, each inner experience he has, will fill the cup a little bit more.

Upon awakening in the morning, the dreamer does a short spiritual exercise where he sees himself drinking the Light and Sound in the cup. He drinks it all.

After he had used this exercise for a while, a strange and interesting thing began to happen. As he visualized the cup, it became brighter. It seemed to have more life. So he finally asked the Inner Master, "What is the golden cup?"

The Mahanta said, "The golden cup is Soul. The more the ECK flows in and out of the cup, the more Soul shines of Its own golden light."

I think you might find this a very helpful spiritual exercise.

83. A Gift for the Master

A dreamer brought an apple to the Mahanta, the Dream Master. But as she brought the gift, she thought to herself, This shouldn't be an apple. I should've brought a peach. A peach, she thought, is a more perfect gift.

As she was holding out the apple to the Master and thinking about the peach she should've brought, she happened to look down. In the Dream Master's hand was a heart.

The woman realized that the form of her gift didn't matter. It didn't matter if she brought an apple or a peach as long as she brought it with her heart.

You can use this as a spiritual exercise. Imagine yourself back in grade school, and bring a gift of some kind to your teacher. If you are an ECKist, you can bring a gift to the Mahanta. If you are of another faith, bring a gift to the teacher of that faith.

Be sure that you are giving with your whole heart. Then your gift will be one of love.

84. Amazing HU

An ECKist was seated in the audience at a major ECK seminar when one of the performers sang a song called "Amazing HU." It was adapted from the public-domain song "Amazing Grace" written in the 1880s by John Newton, the slave trader.

The woman found herself getting very upset with the song. She couldn't understand why she had such a reaction; most of her friends found the new song very uplifting. But instead of hating it, the woman decided to do something positive. She began to memorize all the verses. As she did this, a peculiar thing happened.

The woman began to have a past-life recall of when she was a black slave.

A week later two other ECKists she was acquainted with complained to her about their negative feelings for the song. Without telling them about her experience, she suggested they try memorizing the verses. Right away one of the ECKists had surprising results. He told her, "All of a sudden I was having these memories of when I was a slave in a Native American tribe." Then the woman related her past-life recall as a black slave.

Not long after this, the third person called the ECKist. "Your exercise helped," he said. "I now am able to accept 'Amazing HU,' but I had an interesting experience."

The woman asked, "Did it have anything to do with past lives when you were a slave?"

"As a matter of fact, it did," said the man. He had had a past-life recall of being an Egyptian slave.

The spiritual exercise that the ECKist developed is a good technique for helping you find more spiritual freedom. Perhaps you will have past-life recalls of being the slave, or perhaps you were the slave master. You may learn the times you were taking from life and when you were giving, when you used power and when you used love.

85. Baseball Field

At important times in my life, one of the dream symbols I used to see was a baseball field.

When everything was aligned in proper order and the game was played correctly with a pitcher, a batter, and two opposing teams, that meant my life was in good order. But sometimes the distances between the bases were different and the base path wasn't a perfect square. Maybe from home plate to first base ran from here to forever. Sometimes when I hit the ball, I had to run into the woods to find first base. Sometimes when I hit the ball it would pop and blow feathers all over the place.

If everything about the baseball field was wrong, I would look carefully at my outer life. Something in my life wasn't going right. The sport had gone out of it. There wasn't any fun in it.

It meant I had to work out a plan. I had to discover how to build myself a real baseball field again. I had to get things organized, get the proper space between bases, and get the proper number of players out there. I had to figure out how to play ball. The baseball field was an important dream symbol for me.

As a spiritual exercise you can create your own dictionary of dream symbols that tell you something about your life. Each person's symbols will be unique. Many books on dream study try to use generic symbols that fit everybody. It doesn't work that way.

As you create your own dream dictionary of symbols, put the date beside the current meaning of each symbol. Your symbols will take on new and different meanings as you grow in consciousness.

86. Helping at the Temple of ECK

Here is a spiritual exercise that ties in with the Temple of ECK.

Before you go to sleep at night, shut your eyes and chant HU several times. Imagine yourself at the Temple of ECK in Chanhassen, Minnesota. Ask the Living ECK Master who stands at the door, "What can I do to help at the Temple?"

Imagine yourself cleaning the floor or typing a letter, washing windows or sweeping the floor—whatever you think you'd be good at. You can also try something new. But remember always that you're working in the Temple of ECK.

The Temple of ECK is your own state of consciousness. If you ask me to put you to work, I certainly will.

87. Signing In

An ECK initiate who went to an ECK seminar created a new spiritual exercise during the Sunday-morning HU Song.

In her mind she saw herself with the Mahanta. They were walking into a room through a green doorway which represented the Physical Plane. As they entered the room they saw a table with an ECK Master seated behind it. The Master asked her to sign in.

Signing in meant she was agreeing to enjoy life on the Physical Plane but was also agreeing to go beyond it.

As soon as she had signed the ledger, the Mahanta took her down the hall to another doorway. This one was pink, and it corresponded to the Astral Plane. There was a desk with an ECK Master sitting behind it. Again there was a ledger, and she signed in. This signified her agreement to enjoy life on the Astral Plane but also to go beyond it.

This happened at each plane. On the Mental Plane, she and the Mahanta walked through a blue doorway; on the Etheric Plane, the doorway was a purplish violet. Finally she came to a doorway that was pure white light, the Light of God. She walked through, signed her name in the ledger, and went with the Mahanta to explore this plane.

In your own spiritual exercise, you may travel through the different planes to the Soul Plane. You can visit the Soul Plane with the Mahanta before you are a Fifth Initiate. It's just a visit until you become established there at the Fifth Initiation.

As you practice this exercise, you'll see a change in yourself. Other people might notice it too. With practice, you can become more aware of the spiritual riches you receive on the inner planes of God.

88. One Small Thing for Love

I got a letter from a woman whose life had pretty much caught up with her and stomped her down. She was fed up. In her letter she said, "Harold, tell it to me straight. What do I need to know?"

I wrote back to her, "Do one thing each day for love alone. Don't expect any kind of reward."

When the woman got my letter, she was so excited. She called up her friend, "Hey, Harold actually reads these letters. He wrote back to me!" She wanted her friend to go to the mall with her so she could tell her all about it over tea or a snack. But her friend said, "I can't go to the mall with you; I've got a meeting." So the woman went alone.

She was sitting by an outdoor fountain in a courtyard enjoying her tea. The letter had opened up the love inside her, but there was nobody to share it with. She wanted to spill this love across the table. But the ECK wanted to teach her how to give love in the most humble way.

The woman noticed a small flock of birds hovering around the fountain. Remembering the message I'd given her, she said, "How nice it would be if I had some bread to feed the birds." And just like that, out of the sky came a chunk of bread. Who knows where it came from. It hit her on the shoulder and fell to the ground in front of her. "Heaven does provide," she laughed, and she fed the birds.

After she'd fed them all the bread, her friend walked up. "The meeting was canceled," she said. "We can have lunch after all."

Love gives a shortcut to heaven. The birds couldn't return the woman's love as her friend might have been able to. Her lesson was to do one little thing each day for love and love alone, without any expectation of reward.

If you try this exercise, I think you'll find that life gives you more and more.

89. Spiritual Health

A mother had several children, and one of her sons became very ill. By morning he was better. She told him she needed to go to her room to do a Spiritual Exercise of ECK before work.

She was reading from *The Shariyat-Ki-Sugmad* to use as her contemplation seed, when her son came into the room. "Mother," he said, "may I do the spiritual exercise with you?" And she said, "Sure."

She put a blanket around the two of them, put *The Shariyat* aside, and began to read to him from one of the ECK youth study books. Then they closed their eyes and sang HU together.

During the contemplation she realized that she had been so busy that her child had probably become ill because she hadn't spent enough time with him. She realized that her spiritual health came from her connection with the Mahanta.

And just as the Mahanta cared for her, she also needed to remember to spend time caring for her loved ones. The Mahanta, through the spiritual exercise, was trying to show her how to open herself to the love of God.

90. Initiate Report

So often people who fail say, "I simply cannot deal with my life. Everything is wrong. I just can't get over this problem."

Here is a very simple technique: sit down and write an initiate report.

First, write a few sentences about the problem. Say, "This is what's troubling me. I can't handle it." Then keep writing. Put in some of the experiences you've had that support this problem you're having. Include every detail.

As you write, after about ten or fifteen minutes, you'll find something's lifting from you. Your problem won't be as heavy as it was before.

If the feeling comes back in a day or a week or a month, take time to write about it again. This is one of the steps to self-mastery: learning how to have the discipline to very directly face what's causing you trouble.

If you give this over to the Mahanta in an initiate report or in your dream state, he can take you back and begin unwinding the karma that caused this. No one else can do this for you. You'll be unwinding the real cause of your problem that is making you the flawed spiritual being that you appear to be today but which you do not have to remain.

91. Inside Information

A man used to believe that the spiritual exercises were a kind of duty that you had to do every day. When he wasn't really disciplined, he'd sit down every week or once a month to do a Spiritual Exercise of ECK.

One day he had an experience in which the Master showed him how to make contact with the Voice of God through the spiritual exercises. After that he noticed that life was easier for him. He was able to understand when the Holy Spirit was speaking to him because he now knew a bit about how the Holy Spirit speaks.

This man worked in the investment business as a stockbroker. One day he said to an ECKist friend, "You know, the spiritual exercises are like inside information."

Trading with inside information is illegal in the United States. Inside information is knowledge that a few company officers might have but the general public or stockholders do not have. If someone has inside information he can buy or sell stocks before anyone else.

This man realized that through the inside information we get from the Holy Spirit, our spiritual blessings are multiplied a thousandfold. He now considers the spiritual exercises to be a privilege. The key to the higher understanding of the Holy Spirit comes through the Spiritual Exercises of ECK.

Contemplations . . .

True prayer to God is the kind that says, God, you're doing a good job.

*   *   *

Through the inside information we get from the Holy Spirit, our spiritual blessings are multiplied a thousandfold. The key to the higher understanding of the Holy Spirit comes through the Spiritual Exercises of ECK.

*   *   *

As you practice the spiritual exercises, you'll see a change in yourself. Other people might notice it too. With practice, you can become more aware of the spiritual riches you receive during these exercises of ECK.

*   *   *

Love gives a shortcut to heaven. If you do one little thing each day for love and love alone, without any expectation of reward, you're going to find that life gives you more and more.

*

There won't always be someone to take your troubles away. But if you've taken as much trouble as you need to bear, the spiritual hierarchy sends someone to help you in your hour of need.

Chapter Nine

Health and Healing

92. Guardian Angel

A ten-year-old girl went to the dentist to have a filling replaced. Since a nerve was exposed in her tooth, the dentist put in a temporary filling. In those days, dentistry wasn't very evolved, and the filling wasn't very good. Over the weekend when the dentist's office was closed, the girl's temporary filling fell out.

The exposed nerve caused the girl such great pain that she just lay in bed and cried and cried. Her mother couldn't do anything to calm her down.

That night, long after her mother had gone to bed, the girl felt someone take her hand and just hold it. She fell asleep. When she woke up the next morning, the pain in her tooth was gone. She was able to get through the rest of the weekend and see the dentist on Monday.

The girl later became an ECK initiate and remembered that event. Before she had gone to bed that night, she had prayed to God for help. As a young girl she had believed that a guardian angel had come to her and held her hand, but now she realized it was the ECK Master Rebazar Tarzs.

This is a kind of spiritual healing. There won't always be someone to take your troubles away. But if you've taken as much trouble as you need to bear, the spiritual hierarchy sends someone to

93. Ornade

A woman went to a specialist for a medical condition, and the doctor gave her two prescriptions. The drugs had been very helpful to other patients with the same problem, but for some reason the drugs didn't work for her. Her problem kept getting worse.

One night she had a dream. On the inner she saw a black screen. Suddenly the letters O-R-N-A-D-E appeared on the screen. Each letter was a different color. "Ornade," she said. "What's that?" She had a feeling that whatever it was it would be very significant for her health.

She got up in the middle of the night while the inner experience was fresh and wrote down the name.

The next morning she called the pharmacist who had filled her prescriptions. "Is there a drug called Ornade?" she asked. "Yes," said the pharmacist, "it's often used as a decongestant." He listed a few other symptoms it took care of, but it wasn't used for her particular condition.

In a few days she went to see her doctor again. "The drugs you gave me don't work at all," she told him. "But I would like to try this particular drug," and she told him about Ornade. "I feel kind of foolish telling you this, but I saw the name in a dream."

"It won't work," said the doctor. "It's perfectly useless for your condition." "I'd like to try it anyway," the woman said. Since it wouldn't hurt her, the doctor agreed to write the prescription.

The woman began taking the drug and found to her surprise that it worked very well for her condition. Even though that wasn't what the drug was created for, it took care of her medical problem.

Sometimes the inner message from the Mahanta comes through this clearly, like a sign. But other times, the message comes through in fragments or symbols. Then it depends on the dreamer's perception.

The Spiritual Exercises of ECK help clear out the distortions from your dreams and inner experiences. They allow you to see through the curtain to bring healing to yourself.

94. The Rock Musician and the Muffler

Two brothers have a car-repair show on National Public Radio. For one full hour they try to answer questions from car owners all across America.

The two brothers call themselves the Tappet brothers, Click and Clack—which is the sound the tappet in an engine makes when it's not working quite right. These brothers joke around and make all kinds of fun, but during the course of a call they somehow answer the question in a practical way. They are very creative people.

One day a young man called. He had a problem with his van. He had driven it seventy thousand miles, and the muffler had had to be replaced five times. On a normal automobile, you'd probably only replace the muffler once in seventy thousand miles.

So Click and Clack went at it. They joked back and forth and asked, "Do you take long trips or short trips in your van?" starting the process of elimination. One of the brothers added, "We bet it's short trips." But the caller said, "As a matter of fact, I'm on the highway 80 percent of the time." So that destroyed their theory that the muffler would rust out because of extra moisture from short trips.

The brothers then asked if the young man had replaced the muffler at the same repair shop, thinking that perhaps the local dealer had become upset and given him bad mufflers. But no, the muffler had been replaced at different locations throughout the country.

While one of the brothers talked, the other one sat back and waited. He didn't say anything for a while, then out of the blue he said, "What do you do for a living?"

"I'm a rock musician," the caller said.

"Ah!" said the Tappet brother. "Who do you travel with?" he asked.

"Well," said the caller, "I travel with my band. There are four of us."

"And where do you practice?" the brother asked.

"We practice in our van," said the caller.

"That's your answer," said the Tappet brother. "It's just as clear as can be. The rock music is destroying your muffler."

The rock musician could not handle this. "Come on," he said. "The only way to test your muffler is to play classical music," the Tappet brother answered. "Aw, come on," the caller said again, and he hung up in disgust.

The rock musician didn't realize that this Tappet brother had actually found the right reason for his muffler trouble. Very often the Holy Spirit will use our vehicle—our car or van—to tell us about a health condition, something that is spiritually harmful to us.

People who gossip might find that the mufflers on their cars just go to pieces. A person who becomes angry might have a radiator hose break. The car is saying, you got steamed up!

The Voice of God often speaks to people through something that happens in their outer lives. But few understand Its ways.

95. Monday Sickness

A mother found that when her eldest son was in sixth grade, he was often sick on Monday mornings. The teacher concluded, "He's got school phobia, just send him to school." The doctor said, "Give him these medications, and send him to school." But the mother wanted to find out what the problem really was.

One night in a dream the mother got a nudge to begin checking her son's diet. She recorded what he ate during the week and what he ate on weekends. And she found out he ate more ice cream on the weekends than at any other time.

The mother experimented. She found that when he didn't have ice cream or other milk products on the weekends, he was fine on Monday, ready to go to school. She concluded that he was sensitive to dairy products.

She could've been intimidated by the school officials, who were highly educated. They huffed and puffed and said, "Send him to school anyway." But she said no; she knew there was something else. Because the still small voice of the Mahanta was speaking to her and nudging her to look a little bit further, she found the food sensitivity.

Paying attention to foods can help you lead a better spiritual life. People ask me, "What is good food?" There is no good food or bad food for everyone. It depends upon the individual, upon his particular health condition. Who can best tell what's right for you? You can, of course.

96. Day of Double Miracles

An ECKist mother in Mexico City had a daughter who was having a lot of trouble adjusting to life as a teenager. The daughter had even thought several times of taking her own life. This had caused much pain in the family. So the mother invited her daughter to come to an ECKANKAR seminar, hoping that the talks about ECK would help her.

As the girl listened to the stories of other people who had some evidence of the Light and Sound in their own lives, her eyes grew wider and wider. After the seminar she went up to her mother. "I have found my religion," the girl said. "I am an ECKist."

When the mother and daughter got home, a neighbor came over to hear about the seminar. The neighbor immediately noticed the difference in the young girl. Her eyes were brighter, and she smiled more often. It was as if she had gotten a chance to turn her life around.

The adults were discussing this miracle when the phone rang. The mother went to answer it. Because she had something in her right hand, she picked up the phone with her left. It never occurred to her until she hung up that she had been listening to the phone conversation with her left ear. The doctors had told her that ear was nerve dead; she would never hear on that side again.

But there she was, hearing everything the person on the phone had said.

The mother and daughter realized they had had two spiritual healings that weekend.

People don't get healings every time they go to an ECK seminar. Some people do, some don't. Some do, but never recognize the blessings they receive. For others it may take a week or two. When they're home and they look back on the seminar, they notice something has changed that made their lives better. But healings always depend on the individual: How conscious is that Soul?

97. Light Healing

A girl of twelve had a recurring experience with the Light of God. She'd be in her bedroom at night when suddenly a light would come down the hall toward her room. The light always frightened her. She'd close her eyes, trying to shut the scene from her mind.

After a while she told her parents she couldn't sleep because of the light in the hall. "We'd better take you to a doctor," they said, not understanding.

The doctor prescribed sleeping pills so that the girl could get some rest. Eventually the light went away.

When she was sixteen, she became very sick. The doctor had given her some medicine to take, but she was having a reaction to it and getting sicker and sicker. During the night she called out to her father down the hall to please come to her bedside. But it was late, and her father didn't hear her. So she began to pray to God.

"Dear God," she prayed, "Please come and stay by me. I need your love."

All of a sudden the light she had seen four years before reappeared. Again, it began moving down the hall, but this time she wasn't afraid. The light came into her room and filled her with the most joyful love she had ever felt.

She found herself being pulled out of the human shell. In the Soul form she floated in a world of the most beautiful light and sound. An orchestra played the loveliest music she had ever heard.

When she awoke in bed, her fever was gone. She was healed.

As she got older, she always wondered about this experience with the light. What was that happiness? she wondered. And where can I find it again? One day she told her mother about it.

This time her mother didn't say, "Let's go to the doctor for some more sleeping pills." Instead her mother handed her a book on ECKANKAR. "I think you'll find your answers in here," she said to her daughter.

The light the girl saw was the Inner Master in his Light body, which is a manifestation of the Light of God. It's made of the same spiritual fabric as the cloth of God.

Contemplations...

Our body is a temple of ECK. We must take care of it because it is a house for Soul.

*   *   *

Healings always depend on the individual: How conscious is that Soul?

*   *   *

Paying attention to foods can help you lead a better spiritual life. People ask me, "What is good food?" There is no good food or bad food for everyone. It depends upon the individual, upon his particular health condition. Who can best tell what's right for you? You can, of course.

*   *   *

If you've taken as much trouble as you need to bear, the spiritual hierarchy sends someone to help you in your hour of need. It will be either man or woman, and you can call this individual a guardian angel.

Because he had taken the time to contemplate that morning, the Light of God had come into his heart and was now shining out of his face.

Chapter Ten

The Light and Sound

98. Let Me See Your Pass

An African ECKist was going to work in a building, and as he came to the door, the security guard stopped him. "Do you work here?" the guard said.

"Yes, I do," said the ECKist.

"Let me see your pass," challenged the guard.

The ECKist reached in his wallet and fished around for his pass. Finally he found it and showed it to the guard. The guard was satisfied. As the ECKist was putting his pass back in his wallet, he said to the guard, "You thought I was lying, didn't you?"

The guard said, "No. You just have such a beautiful light in your face. I wanted to talk with you."

Before the ECKist had gone to work that morning, he had done his contemplation as usual. In contemplation, he sat quietly singing HU, allowing the Voice of God to come into him. Because he had taken the time to contemplate that morning, the Light of God had come into his heart and was now shining out of his face.

Sometimes it's just a pleasure to be around someone who's shining with the Light of God. People who aren't in ECK don't always understand what's going on or why this person is drawing them toward him. But there's something special there.

99. Gift of Light and Sound

A Christian woman grew up in a family that was very devout. The mother would get the children up at 5:30 a.m. for prayer. And in the evening at 9:00 they would study the Bible and pray some more. The family believed that everything they needed in life could be handled through prayer.

In 1983 the woman's brother became terminally ill. As he neared the end of his life, right before his passing, he began to speak of a marvelous light that came to him.

"It's so beautiful," he said to his mother and sister. "I can't even put it into words."

The mother said, "Pray to Jesus to heal you."

"He's right here," said the young man. "He's sitting in that chair over there. He's the man who comes to me and takes me into the other worlds to look at this bright light that's too bright to look at. It's brighter than the sun here on earth."

"If I ever recover," he said, "I'm going to get out of the hospital and I'm going to keep looking until I find any information I can about this beautiful light I see in my dreams." But the man died shortly after that.

After her brother died, the woman became somewhat disenchanted with her religion. She was still praying because it was something she'd always done. Soon after that she found a book about

ECKANKAR and came to a crossroads that people often come to before they become a member of ECK. It's a place where you have to say, I cannot follow two paths at the same time; which will I follow?

She decided to do a spiritual exercise. She said, "If there really is a Mahanta, come to me and prove yourself." She went into light contemplation, singing the word HU.

Suddenly in her inner vision she saw the flame of a candle. It began to grow and grow; in the center of the flame stood the Mahanta. He was dressed in light yellow, which signified the Soul Plane. The woman finally realized what her brother had been talking about before he died.

Some of you are fortunate to have conscious experience with the Light and Sound of God. This simply means that you are awakening in the other worlds. What you bring back to earth is more love and a greater understanding of yourself than you had before.

You may try to tell others about this. But most of you will find that unless others have had that experience, they simply won't have any idea at all what you're talking about.

100. Preparing for ECK

A man living in Brooklyn, New York, joined the Pentecostal church in 1967. He wondered very much about God. But as his searchings led to questions, the people in his congregation would tell him, "You don't want to ask too many questions about God. You might get too close to the line where you're blaspheming."

Then they'd reassure him, "Don't worry. All your questions will be answered when you die."

"But I want the answers now," he'd say.

"Have faith the way we do," the leaders of the congregation would say. "All will come to you when you die."

About a year before he left the Pentecostal church, he had an experience with the Light and Sound of God. First he saw a purple and golden light which would stay in his inner vision for about ten minutes if he shut his eyes. Sometimes the purple light became a whirlwind in the distance, coming and going.

He also heard a soft inner sound like crickets. He didn't know what these experiences meant.

So the man asked the people in his church, "What is this Light and what is this Sound that I hear?" The people didn't know; they said, "Don't ask these things. Just be filled with the Holy Ghost."

The goal in that church was to be able to speak in tongues. All these years others in the church had been speaking in tongues, which is a lower form of experience with the Light and Sound of God, a very introductory level. Most people who come to ECK have done this in a past lifetime.

One day the man was sitting in the balcony of his church when the minister said, "Let everyone come forward and witness the Holy Ghost." The man stayed upstairs because he couldn't speak in tongues. So he shut his eyes, and the Blue Light came to him. Then he saw the whirls of purple and gold that he had seen before. The purple light broke and fell like droplets of rain on the congregation. They were receiving the Light of God.

The man was the only one to see the Light; the others felt It. They were on the Astral Plane where the Pentecostal religion makes its heaven.

Not long after that the man found the book *How to Find God* in a bookstore. It explained his experiences with the Light and Sound of God. After more than twenty years in the Pentecostal church he learned that he was having experiences with the Holy Spirit.

There's a religion for every state of consciousness. When you come into ECK, you realize that there is no need to look down on any religious teaching, because at one time you were also a member of that sort of teaching, whether or not it has the same name today.

101. The Balloon Race

A woman had completed two years of study in ECKANKAR. The night before she received her pink slip for the Second Initiation, she had a dream.

In the dream she found herself on a hill speaking with an outcast of society. A crowd stood at the bottom of the hill, watching them. As they talked, the crowd became angrier, more and more judgmental. How dare this ECKist talk with someone they had cast out of their society! the people grumbled.

After they had finished their conversation on the hill, the ECKist suddenly felt she had to flee the crowd, so she ran down the hill and hid in a cave, covering herself with a pile of garments. But the crowd found her and pulled her out of the cave. She found herself face-to-face with the leader of the group. The discussion was pretty much like this: My religion is greater than your religion.

The leader of the group proposed a test. "Let's have a balloon race," he said. "We'll see who can fly the highest." So the ECKist and the religious leader both got into separate hot-air balloons and took off.

As they sailed above the crowd, the ECKist's balloon changed in appearance. It became larger and flew higher than the other balloon, which just skimmed the treetops. But the ECKist flew high and free.

When the race was over, the two came back to the ground. The people on the ground said, "Although we couldn't see the situation clearly, the person from our society won the race. His balloon flew higher and faster." This was exactly the opposite of what was true.

When the dreamer woke up, she realized the meaning of the dream. When she was standing on the hill, she was talking with the Mahanta, who is generally an outcast from society. She felt very keenly the disapproval of the people around her. When she ran away to hide, her peers found her. The two balloons mean the spiritual beliefs of the ECKist and the religious beliefs of the orthodox community. For her, her path was more appropriate because it took her higher. But the others never saw it that way.

This is how it often is in ECK. Even though you know that the Light and Sound of God are substantial and real, other people don't think that way. They don't think of the Light and Sound in terms of actual experience.

Experience is more important than belief. By experience we can know what is true and what is not true.

102. The Atheist

An atheist and his wife were friends with two Higher Initiates in ECK. Although they were close friends, the atheist always thought that the ECKists were making up the things they said about the Light and Sound of God.

The atheist's wife contracted a terminal illness. She became weaker and weaker. One night she was lying in her bed at home, and her husband was holding her hand. He felt the life force leave her, and he knew she had translated. But then the life force returned.

She opened her eyes and said to him, "I have been to a place of light, of such love, where I had perceptions that I have never known before." And as she spoke, he was able to perceive what she had experienced about the living truth, the Light of God in the other worlds.

She lived a short time longer then finally translated. After her death the man began to feel her presence through a feeling of love that hovered nearby. It was as if she had come into this life in part to teach him something about the Light and Sound of God.

Before her death, the man hadn't understood that when we speak of the Light and Sound, we mean a very real, actual experience. We may see the Blue Light, a white light, or sparkling blue lights during contemplation. The light indicates the presence of the Mahanta. It's living proof of his statement "I am always with you."

The Sound can be like the high humming of a generator, the noise of a blender in the kitchen, a bird singing off in the distance, or a flute being played in the same room. These are very real sounds. This is the music of God.

Each time the Light or Sound comes to you, you are lifted in spiritual consciousness.

103. Want Ads

A woman had been unlucky finding jobs; she had gone from one poor-paying job to another. This had gone on for years. It was simply because she had gotten into the job market too late in life and hadn't built up a good history of work experience like those who had started working very young.

One night she said to the Mahanta, the Inner Master, "I need a job where I can help other people, something that would also be fulfilling to me. I need to be in a place where I can give love to others and love doing what I do."

The next morning she looked at the want ads in the local newspaper. She read through different listings but nothing looked good to her. Then a little blue light shone in her inner vision next to one particular ad.

The woman read the ad: "Work half a year for a full year's wages." Usually if something sounds too good to be true, it is, the woman thought. So she kept reading but the blue light stayed on that ad. Finally she said, "Maybe I ought to call and find out what it is."

She called the number listed in the ad. An agency was recruiting a houseparent for several retarded young adults. She went to interview for the job, met the young people, and saw the twinkle of Soul in their eyes. She knew she had found her dream job.

Because she had asked the Inner Master to help her serve and love more, this job had come to her. And the message had come with the Blue Star of ECK, the light pen of the Mahanta. He put her attention on something with just a little spot of light that said, "This is for you. This is for your best spiritual interests right now."

104. Night of the Bells

A story in *Reader's Digest* called "Night of the Bells" was written by a woman who lived on a ranch in South Dakota. The story took place in March, still a very wintry season there. The woman had lost her husband a short time before. One night she woke from a dream at 1:00 a.m., and the sky was light. She wondered, Is it dawn? So she got up and went out on the deck.

The northern lights were flooding the sky in waves of white and blue. The deck had frost on it, so she went back inside and put on her sheepskin moccasins that her husband had made for her. Then she went back outside.

There was less color in the sky than a few minutes before, and she wondered if the show was over. But then the colors grew stronger— reds, greens, and blues. As she stood there and watched the breathtaking display, she realized this was a sacred moment. So she walked up to a nearby hill where she could better see the northern lights. She had often visited that hill since her husband's death.

The woman sat there in her robe and sheepskin moccasins, in the middle of the winter's night. The light show was stronger and more beautiful than before. And then she began to hear, very quietly at first, the sound of tinkling bells.

The bells became stronger when the green

lights glowed, and then they faded away as the lights left the sky. At first the woman thought the bells were glass wind chimes tinkling in the breeze, but she realized there was no wind that night. She remembered that Arctic travelers who had seen the northern lights would also remark on a sound that came when the lights were strong. What is this sound? she wondered.

The woman ended her story saying that none of the scientists she talked to could identify the sound she had heard that night. She concluded that some things are meant to be mysterious. But what she didn't understand was that she was hearing the Voice of God.

The Voice of God comes to people as Sound and Light. When a person is at a certain level in the inner planes, the Sound comes in a certain way. On the Causal Plane, when you are remembering the past, the Sound comes as the tinkling of bells. The woman was missing her husband, remembering the past. At that moment on that very silent night, she was on the Causal Plane, the world where the seed of all karma, all cause and effect, is stored.

105. In One Sentence

An ECKANKAR staff member worked at the Temple of ECK and was often a tour guide. She was on duty one afternoon when a visitor stopped by. He'd picked up some information about ECKANKAR and was curious. "Can you explain this Light and Sound of God in one sentence?" he asked the ECKist.

Nobody had ever asked her to do this before. She was at a loss to explain the Light and Sound of God in a sentence, so she did the best she could in about three or four. But each time she worked as a tour guide, she worried that someone else would ask her such a question. Because she didn't know the answer.

She enjoyed showing visitors a quilt that hung downstairs in the Temple. It had a large golden ᘒ in the center. She explained to them about how love is the creative force that opens your heart. Eventually you become the person with the Golden Heart, where you can experience life in fuller measure than you ever have. You can have more joy and appreciation for life every day.

All of a sudden a message came through from the Inner Master. "The Light and Sound is love in expression," she heard.

The Light and Sound opens the doorway of love. Love is the doorway to spiritual freedom. Before you can realize the gift of spiritual freedom, you must go through that doorway and have the love of God transform your life.

Contemplations . . .

In other teachings, where the Light and Sound is not as direct, it's as if a curtain drops between cause and effect.

* * *

The Light and Sound opens the doorway of love. Love is the doorway to spiritual freedom. Before you can realize the gift of spiritual freedom, you must go through that doorway and have the love of God transform your life.

* * *

Some of you are fortunate to have conscious experience with the Light and Sound of God. This simply means that you are awakening in the other worlds. What you bring back to earth is more love and a greater understanding of yourself than you had before.

* * *

The Blue Star of ECK is the light pen of the Mahanta. He puts your attention on something with just a little spot of light that says, "This is for you. This is for your best spiritual interests right now."

* * *

Even though you know that the Light and Sound of God are substantial and real, other people don't think that way. They don't think of the Light and Sound in terms of actual experience. Experience is more important than belief. By experience we can know what is true and what is not true.

* * *

If your inner life changes to where you have no experience of the Sound or Light, this is very natural, when you understand the cycles of ECK. The quiet period is a time of rest, but it's also a time where you learn to give back to life what you have received inwardly through the Holy Spirit.

* * *

Each time the Light or Sound comes to you, you are lifted in your spiritual consciousness.

The dove is the unenlightened individual. Sweet and pure, but not really understanding the spiritual laws of life. The eagle is Soul, the enlightened Soul. In ECK we like to think of ourselves as eagles, because we are working with the enlightenment of God.

Chapter Eleven

Becoming a Co-worker with God

106. We Come as Eagles, Not as Doves

A Higher Initiate was scheduled to lead an ECK Worship Service in her area. The night before she had been feeling very sick, but she said, "Mahanta, if you can help me get out of bed and to the ECK Worship Service, then I'll do my best from there on." By the next morning she was feeling well enough to go.

She arrived early at the hall and found that the previous occupants had left it dirty. So she scurried around collecting trash and straightening the chairs so that all would be ready for the ECK Worship Service.

Soon the guests began arriving. The Higher Initiate greeted them at the door. One was a Lutheran minister who was looking into other paths.

At the beginning of the service, the Higher Initiate explained about HU, the ancient name for God. Later they had a discussion, and she stayed to talk to anyone who had questions about ECKANKAR.

The minister came up to her and began to chat. Suddenly out of the blue, she said, "We come as eagles, not as doves."

Hearing herself say this startled her a bit, but the minister said, "You know, it's surprising you would say that. I have this recurring dream where an eagle flies me high into the sky on its back. Then it lets me go, and I soar off, free, on my own." The sentence she'd said hadn't made any sense to the Higher Initiate, but it made perfect sense to the minister.

As the woman was preparing to leave, the minister came up to her again. "I want to become a member of ECK," he said. "I'll have someone send you a membership brochure," replied the Higher Initiate, who was tired and wanted to lie down, read her Sunday paper, and relax. But a nagging feeling stayed with her during the car ride home and wouldn't go away.

She knew she had to find the minister a membership brochure right away. It took some searching, but she finally found one inside an old copy of the *ECKANKAR Journal.* Then she got back into her car and drove to the hospital complex where the minister had told her he was working. She went from building to building, asking for him, but no one could help her.

She had tried all the buildings except one, a small house at the wrong end of a one-way street. The street sign said, "Do Not Enter," but she drove down it anyway and rang the doorbell.

The minister opened the door. "How in God's name did you ever find me?" he exclaimed. "Just like that!" she answered.

Sometimes you are called upon by the ECK, the Holy Spirit, to go out of your way to help another person toward the enlightenment of God.

The dove is the unenlightened individual.

Sweet and pure, but not really understanding the spiritual laws of life. The eagle is Soul, the enlightened Soul. Perhaps this is why in ECK we like to think of ourselves as eagles, because we are working with the enlightenment of God.

107. A Talk about ECK

A businesswoman in California got a call one day from a member of a Masonic group. She had given business talks to the group before, and they wanted her to come again. "I'm sorry it's only a week's notice," he apologized. "I would have liked to have given you more time. Is this going to give you enough time to prepare a talk?"

She said yes and agreed to do the talk. After she hung up the phone, she thought it might be an opportunity to give a talk on ECK but not use ECK terms. She knew this group was interested in history. So she decided to put together a talk on kingship beliefs.

As she did her research and put together the talk that week, she realized something wasn't working. Her communication with the Inner Master had stopped; she didn't hear the Sound of ECK. So she decided to go to bed early and set the alarm for 4:00 a.m., a time she felt she was often at her creative best. Maybe something would come through for her talk.

At 2:00 a.m. she was wide awake with a strange feeling of alertness. She'd experienced it before when she was preparing a talk for a regional ECK seminar. Suddenly, the talk for the Masonic group began coming through.

The new title was "How to Get More Out of Your Daily Life: Learning to Recognize and

Understand What Life Is Trying to Teach You." The woman smiled. Here was a way she could talk about ECK to the businessmen without using ECK terms.

The points for the talk just spilled out, one after another: stories from her personal life, waking dreams, things that had happened where the Holy Spirit was telling her something for her spiritual unfoldment. By 5:00 a.m. she had her talk completely written.

In the days that followed, her mind put up arguments as she read over her notes. "Don't try to give a talk like this," her mind said. "You're taking a big risk." The Masonic group was used to hearing her talk about university funds, about generating millions of dollars.

But on the day of the talk she drove to the hall, chanting HU as she went, confident in her material. It felt right. When she arrived, the group was just finishing their luncheon. The person who had called her ran up to her. "We had you scheduled for thirty minutes, but can you do forty?" he asked. As she listened to the business meeting, she got two more waking-dream examples for her talk to fill the extra ten minutes.

As she gave the points in her talk, she noticed first one person in the audience, then another nodding in agreement. When she finished her talk, the group gave her a standing ovation.

What touched her most was a sixty-year-old gentleman who came up to her and said, "I had so many questions, and you've answered many of them. It was fantastic. Could you come back and speak to us again?"

The ECKist didn't have to use the ECK terms to convey the ECK principles. She didn't have to say the words *ECK, SUGMAD,* or *Mahanta.* The group knew she was speaking truth. Some of these people will eventually come to ECK. It's just a matter of time.

108. Cutting the Grass

Before I left for a seminar, it had been raining a lot. I finished my other work a little later than usual, so I finally got a chance to cut the grass right before dark on Sunday night.

In my Minnesota neighborhood you can measure the friction between residents by how much higher or lower the grass is between lawns. A difference of four inches means an anger factor of four in the spiritual weather forecast. People can really get upset if their lawn is cut and yours isn't. So I try to set the standard in my neighborhood.

That Sunday night my next-door neighbor apparently had his television on and didn't hear me start up my mower. He was probably resting up, having made it through the weekend without cutting his grass.

By the time I finished, it was really dark and I couldn't see outside. The mosquitoes were driving me wild. After I put the mower away and went into the kitchen, I told my wife, "Thank goodness that's done. At least we'll have a tidy lawn during the seminar, and we won't get any complaints when we get back."

Suddenly we both heard the sound of a lawnmower starting up next door. My neighbor was out in the dark cutting his lawn.

This is part of the environment of the Temple of ECK. We can reach a certain peak spiritually, but it counts for nothing if you don't cut your lawn.

109. Team Players

A softball team in the Los Angeles area was known as the Soul Travelers. This particular team had lost twenty-three games before they won their first one. It got so that the umpire would say, "These guys are really good losers."

One day the team won a game. They didn't know how it happened. But there it was, a win. They felt the jubilation of victory. And it got them to thinking: Why can't we do this more often?

Depending on whether it's fast pitch or slow pitch, a softball game can be played with either nine or ten players. But each player is an individual. To win, the individuals need to work together.

Sometimes you have a team made up of average players, but together they play exceptionally well. As a team they outplay other teams that have players of a much higher caliber but who are too self-centered to help each other. And so that team loses.

After their first lucky win, the softball team began to win most of their games. They set up rules for working together: (1) do not pick on or criticize any player on the team, (2) don't pick on yourself because that goes against rule number one, (3) practice every week, and (4) sing HU before and after each game. After each game, they would also talk about how they had played and where they could improve.

Because they were winning so much, the next year the league officials put them in a higher division. Now they were competing with even better teams, and they began to lose again. It was like an initiation.

So they went into contemplation to ask, Were they doing something wrong spiritually? Why were they losing all of a sudden?

The Inner Master gave them the answer: "You're doing fine spiritually. You've got to play the game better outwardly."

The team had learned the secret of co-workership, which is the first step. They worked well together. Now they had to concentrate on the details of playing ball. Gradually they were learning how to be better players at a higher level.

The path of ECK means balancing out our individuality with learning how to become a Co-worker with God.

110. Baby Robin

In a tree behind our house lived a family of robins—mother, father, and three babies. One afternoon I was working in the yard when I heard the sound of a very small bird in distress. So I went over to investigate.

As the babies had grown, the nest became crowded. One robin had fallen out; it stood at the base of the tree. The parents were very distressed, yet their instincts said, Feed only the ones in the nest.

I watched for a while to see what would happen. I figured maybe the parents would carry food to the robin that had fallen out of the tree. But the parents never brought it food; it looked as if they were just going to let it starve. I thought about the cat that prowls our neighborhood at night.

As I waited, the baby robin began to peep. It was afraid. It looked up at the nest: it knew where its home was—right there on the end of the branch with leaves on it. But it couldn't get back up; it was too young to know how to fly.

Every so often it would try to tell itself, I'm a big bird, I'm not afraid of anything. Then it would sing the song of a full-grown robin. The peep-peep of the frightened baby bird and the very confident song of the grown robin alternated as the little bird was torn back and forth.

OK, I thought, I've got to do something. I went into the garage and looked around for something to use to pick up the baby robin. A little garden trowel and a stick looked right.

When I approached the bird, it gave me a sour look. "You touch me and I'll . . .," it seemed to say. You'll what, little bird? I inquired silently. I pushed it up onto the trowel with the stick and lifted it up toward the nest.

About this time one of the adult robins came back. It began screeching at me, "Don't touch my baby, please don't hurt my baby," making this big commotion. I was trying to get the little bird into the crowded nest, and it didn't want to go. Its brother and sister spread their feathers to show there wasn't a lot of room.

I nudged the bird with the stick. "This is your only chance," I explained. "If you want to grow up, get in." The bird was looking at me with as much anger as it could muster. It was probably thinking, A steel trowel and an ordinary stick. My word!

Finally I got the little robin into the nest. The others made room for it, and the parent sat on a branch nearby, hopping around, scolding, very nervous. The next day when I went out to check on the bird, all three babies were still in the nest. Two of them looked so innocent, with their little beaks open toward the sky, waiting for Mom and Dad to fly in with another worm. The third baby had his mouth shut and his eyes open, giving me the same sour look as the day before.

"You're not the first one," I told him. "I've helped others and gotten just as much thanks."

The little birds in the nest are like Soul before It finds truth. It's safe and secure in Its small world. Somebody takes care of Its needs, and life is perfect.

Then gradually life becomes less and less perfect as these little creatures grow bigger and it gets crowded in the nest. And there are stirrings within the robins. They say, "Our destiny must be something greater than this nest. We want to go into the world and see if there's something else out there besides worms."

The natural order of life is spiritual unfoldment and growth. Whether anyone likes it, believes in it, or accepts it or not, life says you're going to grow spiritually. Someday you're going to outgrow your state of consciousness. Someday you'll become a Co-worker with God. This is your spiritual destiny.

111. Bean Cake

An African ECKist had a dream where he was in a sports stadium. He was waiting for the Mahanta. But the Mahanta appeared to him not as Wah Z, but as his friend.

His friend handed him a stack of bean cakes. "Take these bean cakes, put them in your pail, and give them to the people in this stadium."

"There are so many people," argued the ECKist. "I need to have more bean cakes."

But the Mahanta in the guise of his friend said, "Take these bean cakes, and give them to the people."

The first group of people the ECKist came to seemed to know he was coming. They were waiting for him. They immediately took the bean cakes he offered.

The second group of people he needed to tap on the shoulder. Then they said, "Oh, yes, we'll have some bean cakes."

The third group of people was even harder to give bean cake to. He tapped them on the shoulder, and still they barely noticed him.

The fourth group was so interested in the game that they had no time for bean cake.

The ECK initiate woke from his dream and wondered what it meant. So he went into contemplation. In contemplation, he saw clearly that his friend was really the Mahanta. Then he realized that the bean cake was food for Soul.

The first group of people were those who were ready for ECK. The second group of people had heard about ECK, but not too much. But once they heard more about it, they were quite interested.

The third group was made up of people who were members of another religion, but they had heard a little about ECK. These people needed a bit more encouragement with the message, or the missionary work of ECK. With the third group the ECK chela knew he needed to use much patience.

The fourth group was so interested in the things of this world or their own religion that they had no use for ECK. To the fourth group, the ECKist gave compassion.

When you go out among people, remember the four different groups of people in this story. Some will be ready for ECK the moment you speak Its name. Others will hear you only when you speak Its name perhaps two times. Still others need to hear it three or more times, but they won't care too much. And the fourth group is not ready for the teachings of ECK at all.

The Master had given the initiate just enough bean cake for all the people who wanted some.

112. It Starts with One

One summer I put out a bird feeder. I'd been noticing birds around the yard and thought it would be nice to have a feeder. So I bought a small bird feeder and a two-pound bag of bird-seed and set the feeder up on the lawn.

How do I find the birds? I wondered. Do I put out a sign? Is it enough to just put out the birdseed?

Periodically I'd check the feeder. By midmorning no birds had come. My wife had a better view from her desk, so I called over, "Any birds by your window?" "No birds," she said.

Then all of a sudden, she said, "There's a sparrow!" I was so excited; I ran over to the window to look, hoping for a pretty songbird of some kind. But there was only a small brown house sparrow.

By the end of the day when I checked the feeder, there was a little group of five to ten birds. By the following morning twenty or thirty birds came to eat at the feeder. Over the next weeks the daily count went up to eighty.

Soon the blackbirds came, then the redwing blackbirds, then cardinals. There were even crows. One night my wife looked outside and saw a gray squirrel climbing on the feeder.

Next I started putting dishes of food on the

lawn underneath the feeder, and the red squirrels came too. My wife saw two rabbits one evening, then two ducks waddled up to the dish.

I had started with two pounds of feed; soon I was buying twenty-five-pound bags. By the next summer I was buying fifty-pound bags of feed to take care of all the visitors that now clamored around the feeder.

Spiritually it's the same way. When you put out the message of ECK, it's like bird feed. First it looks as if no one will come. Then one bird comes and tells another, the same as one Soul tells another. Slowly they come. First the sparrows come; they're not the birds you thought would come but you get used to the idea. Then come the gray squirrels who seem to be pests. These are like the quarrelsome people; you say, "We don't need these people in ECK."

But pretty soon you find you put out a dish of food for them too. It takes more and more feed, but there's always enough money and enough time to find the feed.

You find you get a great deal of love and interest from just looking after the well-being of those Souls who are looking to you for some of their spiritual food.

113. Unseasoned Travelers

A woman from Sweden told me the story of something that happened to her when she was eight years old.

She and her brother went to bed one night. Because the children liked to wander in their sleep, the parents locked the bedroom door.

As the little girl was lying there in the dark, she heard two people come into the room through the locked door. One of them said, "How tired I am!" The other person came over to the girl's bed and touched her on the cheek. "How sweet you are!" said the person. They stayed in the room for a little while, and then they left.

The brother sat up in bed and said, "Who was that?" The little girl didn't know how to answer him, but she knew it wasn't something she had imagined herself because her little brother had heard it all too.

I explained to her that these two visitors were not very high on the spiritual ladder, because they were traveling in the Astral Plane, which is just above the Physical Plane. Travel is very easy for people who live there. You put your thought at the place where you wish to be, and just that quickly you are there.

But those who have newly arrived will walk as they did on earth; and they get tired, because they don't know how to travel by thought. The two travelers were able to walk into the room through the locked door because their vibrations were on a higher level than pure physical objects. They weren't seasoned travelers though.

Almost fifty years later the woman found ECKANKAR. She finally learned what had happened when she was eight and had this experience with the other realms of existence.

114. The Open Meeting

A workshop for Higher Initiates was announced in a region; about ten H.I.'s came. They met at the ECK Center and set up a schedule of activities, including a lunch break.

After a HU Song, the person conducting the workshop said, "The theme for this morning is how to be the right arm of the Mahanta. But we're going to follow a very loose structure and play it by ear."

At 11:30 a.m. they had finished their discussion and decided to go to an early lunch. They weren't scheduled to break for another half hour, but it seemed right to go now. So they went to lunch and came back early.

Just as the Higher Initiates were returning to their workshop, a car drove up and two women got out. They stepped up to the ECK Center and asked if they could come in and participate in whatever was going on.

The Higher Initiates looked at each other for a moment. Then one of them said, "Sure, come on in." So the two women joined the discussion.

They told the group how they had been drawn to the ECK Center. One of the women's son-in-law was very sick with cancer. The doctors held no hope for him. But then a spiritual traveler visited the man in his dreams, telling him about something called the ECK. Through outer treatment with the doctors and these inner visits, the man experienced a miraculous recovery. Later he told his mother-in-law about the dream visitor. When the woman saw the ECKANKAR sign, she wondered if this had anything to do with her son-in-law's experiences.

The second woman had read an ECK book, *In My Soul I Am Free,* about eighteen years ago. It had awakened an interest in different paths of truth. She went from here to there, looking at different teachings. Sometime after that the two women had met each other and become friends.

As the women talked, the Higher Initiates in the group changed the entire structure of the workshop to fit what was happening. Each one of them explained how they had found ECK, and what their experiences had been up to the present day.

The women left soon after; each took an ECKANKAR brochure. And the Higher Initiates marveled at what had happened that day.

"You know," said one of them, "we could've been very self-righteous and told the women this was a closed meeting, that they weren't allowed."

"Yes," said another, "and we could've not listened to the Mahanta when we got the nudge to go to lunch early. Then we would've missed the two visitors."

The Higher Initiates realized that the theme of their workshop had been demonstrated to them. Being a right arm of the Mahanta is serving as a channel for Divine Spirit. It means to be open to the changes that may take place. We, with our minds, set up a schedule, but sometimes the ECK has a whole new plan.

115. Secret Teachings

An ECKist in Africa was an electrical engineer. He had gone to someone's home to do some electrical work. He was working with the son of a very old man who lived there. The son was a retired school principal, up in years too.

The ECKist engineer was telling the son about ECK. As they were talking, the very old man came into the room.

"What are you doing?" he said to the engineer. "What are you doing, telling the secrets of ECK to this child?" This child was the old man's son, the retired principal.

The ECKist said, "They're not secret anymore. In 1965, Paul Twitchell brought them out to the public."

The old man thought awhile. "I first heard about ECKANKAR in 1914," he said. He described the ECK Master who had spoken to him about ECKANKAR. "I see ECKANKAR has finally made it out to this plane," he added.

All these years the old man in Africa had been going to the Temples of Golden Wisdom in the inner worlds to get his teaching about ECKANKAR from an ECK Master with long, blond hair.

The ECKist said, "I'll bring you a picture. I think I know the ECK Master you met."

So the ECKist went home, found his picture of Gopal Das, and brought it to the old man. Gopal Das once served as the Mahanta, the Living ECK Master but now works in the inner worlds.

The old man looked at the picture. "Yes, that is the man who has taught me since I was young, since I first heard of ECKANKAR in 1914," he said.

People today sometimes wonder about ECK. They hear it was founded in 1965 and believe it's something modern. The teachings of ECK have been around for a long time, as this old African man knows.

116. Parking-Lot Hunt

In Minnesota there are a number of very large indoor malls. You can park your car, go in one entrance on the ground level, and come out on the second level. Your car's not there of course, but you can't immediately figure out why.

One weekend I had just narrowly escaped from a group of people at one of these malls who were taking a public-opinion survey. I had let these researchers interview me before, but they had wanted to know all kinds of things I found I didn't care to tell them. "I don't want to answer any more questions," I had said and turned to go.

Another one approached me a few weeks later. I said, "I took the test already," but the person knew all the tricks. "What was it about?" she said. I muttered something and ran for the door.

This time I had avoided them inside and had made it to the parking lot, remembering which level I had parked on. I found my car and was getting in when I noticed a man with a clipboard walking through the parking lot toward me. "My God, is no place on earth sacred?" I said. But he had a strange look on his face.

All of a sudden I realized, This man is not looking for interview victims. This man is lost, or his car is lost, but they're not together. I watched awhile to make sure. He tried to act as if he knew where he was and where he was going. But I noticed he wasn't going anywhere in particular.

So I got in my car and began trying to catch up with him. I realized pretty fast that the best way to catch up with a pedestrian in a parking lot is not with a car. He would cut through the rows, and I would race around to head him off. But as soon as I headed down one aisle, he'd look around like a lost duck and turn in the opposite direction.

Finally I caught up with him. I rolled down my window and called, "Can I help you?" He came up to the window. "Have you lost your car?" I asked him.

"Yes," he said, looking embarrassed.

"It so happens that I lost my car here too once. Which entrance did you walk into?" I said. And he told me.

"See those steps over there?" I said, pointing. "Walk up those steps, and I think you'll find your car." And I explained to him how the shopping mall had several levels.

He was so grateful and happy. He looked inside my car and noticed I had a gadget that secures the steering wheel against theft. "Does that thing really work?" he asked. "I really couldn't tell you," I said. "Every time I come back, my car is still here."

I told him how I had bought it after I got lost in this same parking lot and spent hours one cold rainy night walking around, hunting for my car.

I thought it had been stolen, and that's when I got the idea to buy one of these gadgets. That's when this man got the idea to buy one too.

You learn by experience. But you can also learn from the safeguards another person has taken who's been there before. If you find such a person, and he has a gadget or tool, you might ask about it. Be smart enough to benefit from his experience.

Consciousness allows you to perceive what the ECK is giving you to live this life better. But unless you have opened your heart through singing HU, you won't have the discrimination to know wisdom when you hear it.

117. Hanging Wallpaper

A woman in Florida decided she was going to wallpaper the bedroom as a surprise for her husband. He was going to be out of town for a day or so. She had done wallpapering before and knew it was a very simple job: you cut the wallpaper, put the paste on, and hang it.

But for some reason she had trouble getting the measurements right this time. When she finally got the paper cut and stuck it on the wall, it fell down right away. Pretty soon she was standing ankle-deep in roll after roll of sticky wallpaper. It occurred to her that she should begin to sing HU, just to help out.

The phone rang, and it was a friend she hadn't heard from in a year. "You know what I'm doing these days?" her friend said. "I'm a contractor, and I'm hanging wallpaper." Great, the woman thought with relief, and began to ask her friend for some tips.

When they hung up, the woman went back to her project. With her friend's tips, it began going a little bit better; some of the wallpaper was now sticking to the wall. But the project still wasn't going right. So the woman kept singing HU to herself.

All of a sudden the doorbell rang. The woman opened the door and saw a Jehovah's Witness standing outside. Oh, no! thought the woman. Bad timing.

"I can't talk to you right now," she said to the Jehovah's Witness. "I'm hanging wallpaper."

"Wallpaper!" said the man. "That's my profession." So the woman invited him inside, and he helped her hang the rest of the wallpaper. He had all these tips. They had a nice chat and finished wallpapering the room in no time. She realized the whole project had worked out unexpectedly well.

Because she had asked the ECK for help by singing HU, all this help began to come to her. And it was very specialized help.

I can't say this will happen to you. But I can say that when you sing HU, the Holy Spirit begins to work in your life. It begins to change the situation you're fighting. Maybe you won't see the changes in the world around you, because the problem might not be with your wallpaper. It might be within yourself.

118. Telling Another about ECK

An ECK couple had gone to another city to an ECK event, and when they came home they had houseguests who knew nothing about ECKANKAR. During their conversations with these guests, their recent trip came up. "Yes, we went to this city," said the ECKist, but she never mentioned what they'd been doing there.

After the guests left, the woman felt that she had missed an opportunity. "I had several chances to tell them why we went. I could have told them we were at an ECKANKAR event," she said to her husband. She vowed then to use any opportunity that presented itself in the future.

One day she took her daughter to a park. She was sitting on a bench, watching the little girl play, when a middle-aged woman sat down beside her. They got into a conversation. All of a sudden the ECKist sensed the conversation was taking a turn; it was being lifted to a higher level. She was moving carefully, but she was willing to see if this conversation would go toward spiritual matters.

As they spoke she began throwing in a word here or there about Divine Spirit. And the other woman began using terms such as Zen Buddhism.

Finally the other woman asked, "What is the highest form of creativity?" From inside the ECKist came the answer, "Being positive is the highest form of creativity I know."

This was exactly what the middle-aged woman needed to hear. The way the ECKist phrased the sentence meant something to this woman.

ECKists have answers to questions like What happens after this life? or What is the Holy Spirit and how does It work? or What is the nature of God? But just because you are in ECKANKAR doesn't mean you have the best understanding of those answers. You, yourself, may learn from the person who knows nothing about ECK but is a living example of the principles.

119. Giant Utensils of Heaven and Hell

A wise man died one day. Although he was very wise, he had done some minor infraction while on earth, and for this he was obliged to spend a short time in hell.

When he arrived, he was quite surprised. He found the furniture was in good condition, even modern. There were tables laden with all kinds of food. And the temperature was just right—not too hot and not too cold. "I wonder why they call this hell," he mused.

When it came time to eat, he found out. All the eating utensils were six feet long. The law of hell required that all the people there use the utensils if they wanted to eat. They had the most difficult time trying to get the huge fork or spoon to their mouths. Even though there was an abundance of food, the people in hell were starved and emaciated.

Time passed, and this person had spent enough time in hell. He had worked out his sentence, and the powers that be said, "All right, you may now go to heaven."

So the wise man came to heaven, and he was very surprised to find out how things were there. The furniture was brand new, the same as in hell. The temperature was just right, the same as in hell. And there were tables laden with food. But then he saw the utensils. "Oh no!" he said.

"They've got these six-foot-long utensils for eating here too!"

But when he looked around, he saw that the people were all healthy looking; they had nice, plump faces, and they were happy and laughing. And he said, "Everything here is the same as in hell. Why are all the people so happy?"

The gong sounded for dinner, and all the people began to eat. But instead of trying to feed themselves, they took up the long utensils and began to feed each other.

This is the principle of becoming a Co-worker with God. There are two aspects of the path of ECK. The first aspect is Soul as the individual. We are each a unique divine particle of God. The other principle is this: for individuals to become spiritual, they must become Co-workers with God. This means to serve others.

Keep the parable about the giant utensils of heaven and hell in mind as you go out into the world to get your spiritual food.

Contemplations . . .

Sometimes you are called upon by the ECK, the Holy Spirit, to go out of your way to help another person toward the enlightenment of God.

* * *

God's Word is not hidden or contained in the office of the clergy. The Word of God is in the heart of each of you.

* * *

You find you get a great deal of love and interest from just looking after the well-being of the Souls who are looking to you for some of their spiritual food.

* * *

It's a pleasure to be around someone who's shining with the Light of God. People who aren't in ECK don't always understand what's going on, or why this person is drawing them toward him. But there's something special there.

* * *

The natural order of life is spiritual unfoldment and growth. Whether anyone likes it, believes in it, or accepts it or not, life says you're going to grow spiritually. Someday you're going to outgrow your state of consciousness. Then you can become a Co-worker with God. This is your spiritual destiny.

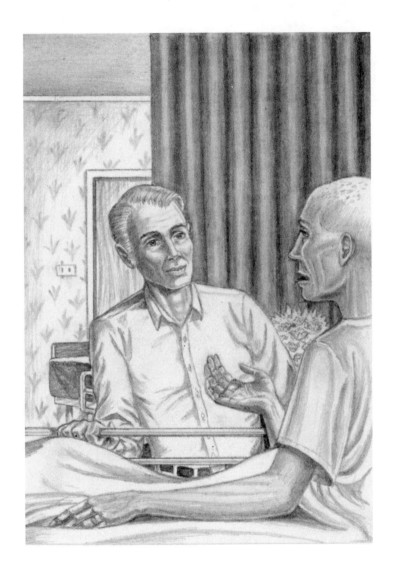

Look for the divine nature that exists in other people as well as in ourselves.

Chapter Twelve

Tips for Mastership

120. Chatter

A hospice volunteer had offered to visit with a terminal patient who had a brain tumor. The hospice worker visited once or twice a week for two hours. The patient had been talkative before his illness, but now he went on nonstop, chattering like a blue jay from the beginning of their meeting to the end.

The ECKist never had a chance to give him any kind of spiritual help, to tell him about the HU. This worried the ECKist because the man was so close to translating. But most of all it tired him. In fact, it got so bad that the ECKist often came home from his volunteer work totally exhausted.

One night in contemplation he asked the Mahanta, "Is there anything you can do about that man's constant chatter? It's really becoming difficult to bear."

The Master said, "You only have to listen to his chatter for two hours, twice a week. I have to listen to you nearly twenty-four hours a day."

The answer surprised the ECKist. He began to see the lesson in his experience with the terminal patient. But he wondered, Was listening enough? Shouldn't he be telling the man about HU?

Not long after that the man translated. That evening, the ECKist came home very tired from working his night shift. He decided to go to bed earlier than usual. While he was asleep, the Mahanta took him out in the Soul body to view the translation of the patient in the hospital.

When he saw the patient on the inner at the moment of his translation, the man had such a look of happy surprise on his face that the ECKist was relieved.

He realized that the ECK had been working with the patient all along. This cycle for this Soul had been completed. All the ECKist had had to do to help this Soul along was simply live the life of ECK with love, to recognize the divinity in himself and in this other Soul.

In ECK we are taught to look for the divine nature that exists in other people as well as in ourselves.

121. The Silver Dollar

An eight-year-old boy lived on the East Coast where his parents had a rooming house. One day a traveler came through. The man was kind of an interesting person, but he seemed to be down on his luck.

The boy had just received a silver dollar for his birthday. His uncle had given it to him, saying, "Keep this silver dollar; it's special. It will grow more valuable as time goes on." The boy put the silver dollar in his room.

One day the boy was outside playing when the traveler sat down on the stoop beside him. They talked a little bit, and the boy noticed how careworn the traveler seemed, although he never asked for help or money. The boy felt he wanted to do something for this man, so he said, "Just a minute," and ran inside to get his silver dollar. He came back out and gave it to the man.

The man took the silver dollar and held it between his fingers. He said, "This is very special to you, isn't it?" and the boy said, "Yes, it is." The man said, "Are you sure you want to give it to me?" "Yes, because you need it more than I do," the boy answered. So the man took the silver dollar.

The man became friends with the boy, and the two would often sit outside on the stoop playing checkers. "This game is like life," the man

351

would tell the boy. "Look where you moved. You knew what you wanted to do, but you also have to know what I'm going to do with any of these other pieces." The traveler was teaching the boy the Law of Karma, of cause and effect. "When you move your pieces, notice how you box yourself into a corner."

As luck would have it, weeks after the traveler left for another city, his mother was talking with a visiting relative and called to the boy, "Come bring your silver dollar to show your aunt." All of a sudden the little boy's heart froze, and he didn't know what to do. He said to his mother, "I don't have the silver dollar. I gave it to the man."

"You gave your silver dollar to a bum?" she screamed. She scolded him for being such a fool, even though his heart had told him that the gift of the silver dollar would mean so much to the man who needed it more. Now his mother was saying he had done wrong. He felt very bad.

A few weeks later, the boy had a dream. In the dream the man came to him. He pulled out a silver dollar and held it up to the boy. "Remember this?" he asked. The boy said, "Yes, it's the one I gave you." The man said, "It's very precious, isn't it?" The boy nodded, because after his mother's scolding, he knew just how precious it was.

So the man put the silver dollar into the boy's hands in the dream. He said, "Now hold tight," and the boy held it to himself. He could feel the silver dollar in his hand. Then he woke up.

help you in your hour of need. It will be either a man or woman, and you can call this individual a guardian angel.

As he became aware of his body lying in the bed, he felt something very hard in his hand. He opened his hand and looked, and there was the silver dollar. The man in his dream had given back his silver dollar. And the child accepted this.

The years passed, and just about the time that Paul Twitchell translated in 1971, the young man came into ECKANKAR. He just missed seeing Paul. But one day he found a book with Paul's picture on it. "This is the man who stayed in my mother's rooming house when I was a child," he said. "This is the man I gave my silver dollar to, and who gave it back to me in the dream."

On the twenty-fifth anniversary of the founding of ECKANKAR, the man was invited to the Temple of ECK for its dedication. He walked downstairs to some of the empty rooms on the ground floor, thinking about a visit he had made six months earlier when the Temple was still under construction. At that time, the man had taken his silver dollar and pressed it into the earth in one of the rooms of the Temple.

As he stood in the same room on the day of the dedication, thinking about all the experiences he had had with the silver dollar, the wall began to shimmer. Out of the shimmer of light came a group of ECK Masters. They passed through the room and went upstairs to where the dedication was to take place. The last one to enter the room was Paul Twitchell. Paul walked over to the wall and stared at it for a while. "Hmmm, better than I imagined," said Paul, then he walked out of the room.

The silver dollar was placed in the Temple with love. It was put there by someone who had learned many lessons from a simple silver dollar. The lessons went all the way back to the founder of ECKANKAR, Paul Twitchell, who taught the boy something about life when Paul was on his own way to Mastership.

122. High Score

Video arcades are quite a big thing in Minneapolis. There are teenagers in there, and there are people in their thirties and forties. It's a place where people come to forget their troubles and show their children a good time.

I was standing in front of a game I play a lot. On this game you can play a long time on one token. It's called Ms. Pac-Man. My score was getting up there in the higher ranges.

Four twelve-year-old girls had gathered around, watching me. They got caught up in the game when they saw Ms. Pac-Man barely getting ahead of the monsters.

"Listen," I told them, "I'm going to go up to a certain score, and then I'm going to quit and you can have the rest of the plays." So they said they'd wait.

In the meantime two young men came over. They were about fourteen or fifteen, a little older than the girls. One of them stood to my left and bragged, "I can get a better game than that anytime!"

It looks easy when you're watching someone else. This guy talked on and on, and eventually he drove the girls away. Then he tried to impress his buddy. "I'm from Detroit," he said. "I can turn that machine over three, four times." Turning it over means getting the highest possible score on the machine.

So I got kind of adventuresome. I asked him, "What kind of a score are you talking about?" He told me all these things about how he can get such a high score. So I said, "Great! You sound like a really good player. I'll let you have this game so you can show me."

The fellow started backing off. I ran Ms. Pac-Man right into a monster, and he couldn't believe it. "Hey, don't do that!" he said. "I'm giving you the game," I told him. "I want to watch you play. There's a free token in the machine, and I'll let you have it."

So he got up to the machine, feeling really important. His buddy moved in on the side. As he started playing, he immediately ran right into a monster. Then he did it again. In about two minutes, he had lost all his plays and had such a low score that even a rank beginner would be embarrassed. It was just over a thousand points.

"I'm going to the money changer and get some more tokens," he told me. I thought, That's nice for the place. Up until now he had just stood there and talked. After he came back I watched him a few more minutes. When he went to the token machine again, his friend turned to me and said, "I can do a lot better than he does. By the way, what was your high score?"

I said, "553,000. But I usually don't do it because it takes too long."

The first guy came back and I heard them

talking very quietly. One said, "He says he had 553,000." "I can do better," said the other, and I knew I had nothing to learn from them. So I walked off.

These two people were a perfect example to me of individuals who are so filled with themselves that they would never be able to hear the Voice of God speaking to them. If you can't hear the Voice of God speaking to you in little things, how are you going to hear It speaking to you in big things?

123.   Motorcycle Man

A young girl began having experiences with someone she'd call the motorcycle man. She was about three or four, still in her crib.

Every night just before she'd go to sleep, she'd hear a motorcycle driving along the street. It would drive to the front door and down the steps to the basement. There it would wait, its motor humming very quietly.

A man would come up the stairs while she was still awake. As soon as he'd come into the room, the girl would shut her eyes because she was afraid. But even though she had her eyes shut, she could still see things as Soul. For some reason, as soon as she shut her physical eyes, the fear would go away.

The motorcycle man would come into the girl's room and ask her, "Want to go for a ride on the motorcycle?" And being a kid, she'd say, "Sure."

So she and the kindly man got on the motorcycle and rode out of the basement. They'd go on all kinds of adventures. This went on for a couple of years.

The next morning she'd tell her parents, "The motorcycle man gave me a ride again last night." Her parents would say, "You were only dreaming." But the girl knew it was more than a dream.

Years later she came across a book about ECKANKAR and knew that her experiences had been with an ECK Master.

The spiritual travelers try to help people of any age explore the inner worlds, so that these people may also have more wisdom and freedom. This is part of the package of God Consciousness: to be fully, universally aware of your own worlds at all hours of the day and night.

124. Power or Love?

A Higher Initiate went into contemplation and asked the Inner Master, "How do you find the time to take care of the needs of all beings?" Instead of giving her a direct answer, the Inner Master gave her a vision.

Taken out of the body through Soul Travel, the woman looked down upon a scene. A school bus was traveling down a country lane. At a crossroads, the bus stopped. A child got out and began to run toward home.

The child was passing through a forest area when the Higher Initiate saw a wolf stalking the girl. The Higher Initiate said to the Mahanta, "Can you protect the child, so the wolf doesn't eat her?"

So the Master let a rabbit run in front of the wolf. The wolf went after the rabbit, and the child reached home safely.

When she saw how things had turned out, the Higher Initiate felt uneasy. "Did it have to be a bunny?" she asked the Inner Master.

The Master replied, "Life is choice. One choice, then another choice, then another. What is the difference if I provide a rabbit for the family's dinner or if I provide the same rabbit for the wolf's dinner? Everything has needs, and there's always a choice. In this case the choice was the freedom and welfare of the child."

This awesome power of life and death is the same power that every Soul has. A power to use or abuse.

Power without love creates people like Hitler. The pure balance of the Holy Spirit is power and love, but mostly love—God's love. This is what we are trying to develop for ourselves.

125. Key of Opportunity

Two weeks ago, I was in the post office getting my mail. A father came in with his daughter. She was really small, and in her hand she held a key.

The child ran back and forth across the lobby, trying her key in all the different mailboxes that lined the room. I went over to my box and put my key in to get the mail out. The little girl came over and stood beside me, watching. She thought it was very interesting: My key worked when hers hadn't.

I shut my mailbox, and the father scooped up his little girl and started out the door. He said to me, "When you're this age and you've got a key, the whole world is a lock." We both laughed at this.

Later I was thinking about what he had said, trying to unlock the spiritual meaning. I realized that for a child the whole world is an opportunity. It's something to unlock. The child is always asking life, "Will my key work here?"

It's this childlike attitude—that the whole world is an opportunity—that makes life a joy to live.

126. Heart Learning

In an ECK Satsang class in New York, the students were studying the attributes of God Consciousness. Each brought in an example to share with the others.

One woman related a story about an ECKist who'd been knocked off the sidewalk by a taxicab. The fall had broken her arm. In just seconds a crowd had gathered, wanting to take the cabdriver apart. They urged her to sue and get some money for her injury. But the woman had felt sorry for the cabbie. She preferred to take her lessons in spiritual value and not in money.

The class member said to the others, "To me, this is a person who shows the quality of God Consciousness. Her love was so great that she was more considerate of others than she was concerned about her own bad situation."

After class the ECKist planned to take a train home. She was pretty hungry. All she had was her token for the train fare and three dollars. She figured it was just enough to buy a sandwich in one of the shops at the train station.

She got herself a chicken sandwich and went out on the platform to wait for her train, still thinking about the qualities of God Consciousness, so happy that she had been able to contribute to the discussion that evening.

As she stood there a disheveled man approached her. "Please, I'm hungry," he said. "Can you give me some money for food?" She knew she didn't have money, but she did have the chicken sandwich. She thought long and hard, then she handed it to the man. "Here, you can have this if you're hungry," she said. This was more of a sacrifice to her than if she had given him twenty dollars. What she had to give up was most dear to her.

This is how the teachings in ECK usually come. You're on a train platform at night, cold and hungry and tired. Someone comes up to you and says, "Please, give me that which is most precious to you." She had to put aside her initial reaction to the disheveled man and recognize the spiritual experience that was before her.

The Master, in effect, was telling her, "You've got the mental knowledge, the head learning, about a quality of God Consciousness. Now we're going to practice it so it becomes part of your heart."

127. The Pilgrims

A crowd was gathered in a mountainous area on the inner planes. They were seeing a group of pilgrims off on a journey. The pilgrims were taking a long, dangerous trip through the mountains to a holy place, a sanctuary of wisdom where they felt they could get wisdom that they couldn't get where they were at their present time.

The crowd applauded the pilgrims. "Look at them go. Good luck to you! Have a wonderful time," they cheered.

So the leader of the pilgrims turned to the crowd. Very sternly he said, "You must meditate more." The crowd was happy, enjoying themselves, but the leader was essentially saying, "We are more holy than you. Even though you aren't coming on this sacred pilgrimage, at least follow our example and meditate more." That was his message. And then the little band went off.

I stood in this crowd watching the pilgrims go off on this long, hard journey. It would take them along winding mountain paths, up and down. And I remembered an earlier group that had gone on a similar pilgrimage a couple of years ago. After months and months, one or two stragglers had come back. "It wasn't there," they said. "It wasn't there."

They had realized that wherever they walked was holy ground. Heaven isn't a place, it's a state of consciousness. This is where you go in your dreams. You go to heaven, but you go there in a state of consciousness where you wear a body, see people who are doing things, and participate in an active way.

It's not important what's there. What is important is what you learn from being there.

128. Zelda

Between meetings at a seminar, I was eating lunch with a few friends. Of course, being at an ECK seminar, we talk of highly spiritual things. "What's happening in the video arcades lately?" I asked them. "I've noticed in the last few years that fewer people are going in."

"That's because the home video games are getting better," one person said. "They're very interactive and instructive. There are some really good games, like Zelda II: The Legend of Link."

He went on to describe the game. The hero in this computer game is called Link. Link goes through all these worlds, from level to level. He meets a lot of obstacles. Sometimes a wall blocks his way. If Link does something to the wall, like find a secret passageway, he can move to the next level.

Whether the game is won or lost depends on if Link has the right tool for each obstacle that confronts him. If he knows which tool to bring with him or where the tool is hidden on that level, he can use it to get past the obstacle. Tools he discovers on one level he may not be able to use right away, but if he keeps them, he'll be able to use them on the next level.

The game is very much the same as the spiritual experience of reincarnation. In each of our incarnations, we learn a particular lesson or develop a certain skill. As we go into succeeding lifetimes, we need the tools that we have mastered. But we have often forgotten them.

The way the average person outside of ECK has to get the right tool is by reincarnation. It's a very slow process.

If only we could tap into our total experience as Soul, draw upon what we learned last time around, and bring it into this lifetime. It could help us solve a problem that's holding us back on the spiritual path. By not using our full collection of tools, we prevent ourselves from moving to the next level of the game of life.

The reason I'm teaching dream travel and Soul Travel is this: If you run into a block in this life that prevents you from going to the next level or the next initiation, you can go back through Soul Travel or the dream state. You can go back to a past life and pick up the tool or talent that you need and bring it into the present.

Sometime in the far future some psychologist will make a study of this. He might say that the people who create games like Zelda actually have a very deep insight into life.

129. The Mime

In Australia I was walking along the city streets when I saw a small crowd gathered around a man with a suitcase. He was a mime. In a very creative way, he had built his audience out of nothing, just by stopping the mechanical flow of the crowd that passed by him.

The mime had put down his suitcase in the middle of the sidewalk. This became his stage. He put on a comical hat, a funny-looking coat, and clownish glasses. Then he would pick a pedestrian to mimic.

One pedestrian who walked by had on a floppy hat with the brim turned down. A sour look sat on his face as he stomped along, head down. The mime fell into step behind him and for a few minutes perfectly aped this man's manner of walking.

When the pedestrian caught him at it and began to turn around, the mime started turning around too. They both kept turning around; the audience thought it was extremely funny. Then the pedestrian realized what was happening and quickly got out of the mime's stage.

Next the mime saw a young woman hurrying by with mechanical motions, very much like the human level of consciousness. The mime fell at her feet like a lover. He motioned that she was the most beautiful woman on earth. As he was hugging her feet, he happened to take off one of her shoes. She stood on the sidewalk, embarrassed and laughing with one shoe off, as he cradled her other shoe. Then he put his nose in it, took one sniff, and immediately passed out. The crowd loved that.

After he did this routine for a while, I noticed how the river of people had changed. Now there was a small lake of people standing off on the side, watching. They were part of his audience. Every trait he mimicked was common to one of the watchers, and therefore everyone could laugh. And the people watching felt a common element of humanity.

This street artist was pointing out a basic truth: We are all Soul. And we are actually pretty funny-looking human beings when we get caught up in ourselves.

The mime was being a messenger for God to break up the mechanical marching of the human consciousness.

130. Secrets of Mastership

On the inner planes I was walking through the streets of a town in the manufacturing area. Two young boys came running after me; they were about ten or eleven. One called to me, "Can we come along with you?"

"Sure," I said.

We came to a huge warehouse, big enough to hold the Goodyear blimp. As soon as we went in, the boys began to jump around excitedly with a kind of joy. There was real freedom in this place.

"Do you know why you have this sense of freedom?" I asked them. They shook their heads; they didn't know. I said, "Look at the people in here."

For the first time, they looked around. The entire building was filled with craftspeople, experts in their fields. There were master carpenters, master plumbers, computer operators, interior designers, artisans, and artists. They were remodeling the warehouse and creating things for people.

"Look at these people," I said again. "Each is an expert. They come here to do whatever they do better than anyone else. They get their satisfaction in life from doing a job well. Buyers come here expecting the finest, and they get it."

A young man in his midtwenties came walking by. He said, "I overheard you talking about what it takes to attain mastership and spiritual freedom," he said. "What did you do when you worked in a production phase like this?"

"I worked in printing," I said. "But whether it's printing or another craft, learning how to be careful and exact with what you do is the key. Do it for the love of God and not for the love of money."

I told the two young boys to come back again tomorrow, to watch the craftspeople at work. If the boys care enough about a task, some craftsperson might show them the secrets of how to become a master in that area.

These people were living spiritual freedom. And the first step to attaining this freedom is learning how to do something well because you love it, not because you're being paid to do it.

The lesson of the warehouse and the spirit of freedom that the young boys felt is this: Become an expert in something. You need to be grounded in something. When you do something for God, for the highest principle, you do each step until it sings.

Mastership is anything except just getting by.

131. Ray's Long Journey of Many Seasons

On a flight to Australia, my seat companion was a tall guy who looked a little like the comedian Jerry Lewis. He was grumping and grousing as he got into his seat by the window, but he was the kind of person you didn't feel offended by, even when he spoke that way.

"Hi," he said. "My name is Ray." My wife and I introduced ourselves. "They have us crammed in here like cattle," he went on. "If you want to pay more money than the flight's worth, you could sit up in First Class."

As we began to talk, it turned out that this man had seen many hard things. He had been born on Saturday, December 13. He had missed Friday the thirteenth by one day, he said, and after that his life had gone downhill.

He was drafted into the Army as one of the first soldiers sent to Vietnam. The letter came on April Fools' Day. He served as a foot soldier, then as a cook for a while. When his time was up, he asked to be transferred back to the field as a cook because he wanted to give the new soldiers who were coming in good food. "I never got good food like that," he said. He somehow managed to find a friend with a helicopter and got steaks for the men.

When he got out of the Army, he lived in a

trailer court and bought a Corvette he'd always wanted. Soon after he moved in, a gunfight broke out in the neighboring trailer. "Wherever I go," he said, "things happen." Ray's whole life had been one strange experience after another.

He worked for the fire department of his city, plus ran a couple of part-time jobs, at a car-rental agency and others. It was a small car-rental agency, so the only way they could compete for business was to provide something special. Ray dreamed up the idea of picking the customer up at the airport, and filling out the paperwork for them ahead of time. Businesspeople traveling through that city loved it; they began to ask for Ray.

Here was one of these people traveling a long journey of many seasons. He had no idea what it was about, why he was getting these experiences. It's simply Soul going through life, because Soul has heard the Sound of God.

I found it very interesting that Ray didn't surrender to these supposed negative forces in his life. He didn't give up. No matter what he did, Ray always did the very best he could. He never settled for less.

132. A Focus on God

A staff member of ECKANKAR who works at the ECK Temple has a cat she calls Calamity Jane. The cat usually comes in at 10:30 at night and brings her owner a mouse as a gift.

One night the cat didn't come in until 5:00 a.m. When the owner looked at the doorstep, there were two mice lying there as an apology. The ECKist was happy her cat was back, but she felt kind of sad about the mice. She'd prefer the mice be running free somewhere else.

Later that week she was talking to a friend. The friend asked, "I wonder why it is so easy for a cat to catch mice?"

The owner suddenly had a mental image of Calamity Jane stalking a mouse. "If you've ever watched a cat stalk a mouse," she said to her friend, "you'd see that every fiber of its being is focused on the mouse."

Then the ECKist thought, If we could just focus for one minute on something important, just think how wonderful that would be, especially if our focus was on God. Then out of her mouth came the words, "Focus on God the way a cat focuses on the hunt."

The ECKist had recently been wondering how she could move farther along in her spiritual life. Sometimes God or a better life is so close, we simply can't recognize it.

133. The Locksmith

An ECKist was in charge of the ECK Center one Friday evening. This center had several rooms leading to an inner room. By some chance, as she walked out of the inner room, she locked the door behind her. Later she discovered her car keys were still in the inner room.

She called another ECKist who lived nearby. "I've locked my car keys in the inner room," she said. "Can you bring your keys and open the door?"

The other ECKist arrived and tried both of his keys to the ECK Center, but none of them would open the inner door. So they stood there, trying to think of ways to get in.

"We could break a window," he said. "No," she said, "we could break down the door." "Why don't I use my credit card to open the lock?" he offered. "I've seen it done in movies." But the man's credit card was too stiff to go around the door frame.

So they went through the office building and found the custodian. "I'm sorry, I can't help you," he said. "I just have the keys to let people into the building, but I don't have keys for any of the inner rooms."

Then one of them thought of the obvious solution: Why not call a locksmith? They looked through the Yellow Pages and found a twenty-four-hour locksmith. In no time at all he was there.

The locksmith had all kinds of tools for picking locks. He tried a few of them, then reached into his wallet and got out a credit card. It was flexible enough to spring the lock.

Later the ECKist was driving home, thinking about what had happened. "The inner room holds the secrets of the heart," she said. "In there are my keys so that I can go home—to God, of course."

When the two tried to open the door, they had first put their minds to it, thinking of rather crude ways like breaking a window or breaking down the door. They tried their own credit card, but it was too stiff and wouldn't bend. Then they went to the custodian, who represented the ruler of the lower worlds, Kal or Satan. He only had the keys for outer doors, like the earth plane.

So they called the locksmith, who represented the Mahanta. He was available twenty-four hours a day. He had all the right tools, but he used a simple credit card.

The only difference was that his was more flexible.

The Mahanta often uses the same talents you have, but he shows you in a more flexible way how to use your talents yourself. The difference between the Mahanta and a savior of another religion is this: The savior tries to save you from yourself, and the Mahanta tries to help you help yourself.

134. The Jade Master

This is the story of the jade master. It's in a
book by Ed Seykota called *The Trader's Window*. It
is about a young man of nineteen who was
puzzled; he didn't know what to do with his life.
One day he heard of a jade master who lived
about five miles away. So the young man said to
himself, Even though it's winter and a five-mile
walk, I'm going to go to the jade master and learn
all about jade.

So he walked five miles through the snow in
the bitter cold. He came to the jade master's house
and knocked on the door. An old man opened
the door; he had a broom in his hand. "What can
I do for you?" he said.

The young man said, "Are you the jade master?"

The old man nodded.

"I've come to learn about jade. Would you
take me as your student?"

The old man said, "Come on in."

When the young man came inside, the jade
master made him a cup of green tea. As he was
ready to serve the tea, the jade master pressed a
green stone into the young man's hand. "Hold
that while we talk," he instructed. And as they
sipped their tea on this cold winter's day, the old
man began telling a story about a green tree frog.

After a while the young man became impatient. He had come here to learn about jade; he didn't care about tree frogs. So he said to the old man, "Excuse me. I came here to learn about jade."

The old man looked at him for a moment. "Oh, excuse me," he said. "Why don't you come back next week?"

The young man was puzzled, but he agreed. He walked the five miles through the cold snow, got all the way home, and about a week later repeated the trip. The old man greeted him enthusiastically, ushered him into the room, and made him a cup of green tea. Before they began to talk the old man again pressed a green stone into the young man's hand.

The young man had high expectations of learning about jade that day, but the old man launched into the same story about the green tree frog that he had told last time. The young man was able to contain his impatience and listen a little longer, but finally he couldn't stand it anymore.

"Excuse me, excuse me," he interrupted, thinking the old man was going senile on him. "I came here to learn about jade."

The old man looked at him again, then said, "Maybe you'd better just go home and come back next week."

This went on all winter long. But each time, the young man interrupted less and listened longer. Finally when spring came, the young man had learned a couple of things. He had learned how to make green tea and sweep the kitchen with a broom. He had learned to make himself useful doing all the things that needed to be done, because he had become a friend of the old man.

When the old man sat down and started talking about the green tree frog, the young man could just listen now. He would just sit there and listen and never interrupt. And the next week he would come back through the snow again.

One day when he came for his weekly visit, the old man was waiting at the door. It was spring now, much easier weather for making a visit to the jade master. The young man went inside. The old man had the tea ready for him, and they sat down. The old man pressed a green stone into his hand the same as usual and gave him a cup of tea. Then he began to tell the story about the green tree frog.

Suddenly the young man said, "Wait a minute. This isn't jade." He suddenly knew that the green stone in his hand wasn't jade.

Like the jade master, the Mahanta, the Living ECK Master gives us a precious gem, the HU. He presses it into our hand, but we must take it into our heart and make it a part of our life. Then we can know truth.

Contemplations . . .

We would often like to carry the sorrows of others because they seem lighter than our own. But as we work out our karma, the ECK often makes us go over a road that is rocky for us in ways that no one else knows. Because it's our own road.

* * *

Whenever I see people moving toward the polarity of power, I foresee all the problems they're going to cause, first for others and finally for themselves. But if I see an individual going along the path of love, I see a bright future for the person.

* * *

Heaven isn't a place, it's a state of consciousness. This is where you go in your dreams. You go to heaven, but you go there in a state of consciousness where you wear a body, see people who are doing things, and participate in an active way.

* * *

In ECK we are taught to look for the divine nature that exists in other people as well as in ourselves.

*　*　*

Become an expert in something. You need to be grounded in something. When you do something for God, for the highest principle, you do each step until it sings. Mastership is anything except just getting by.

*　*　*

The difference between the Mahanta and a savior of another religion is this: The savior tries to save you from yourself, and the Mahanta tries to help you help yourself.

*　*　*

Like the jade master, the Mahanta, the Living ECK Master gives us a precious gem, the HU. He presses it into our hand, but we must take it into our heart and make it a part of our life. Then we can know truth.

Glossary

Words set in SMALL CAPS are defined elsewhere in this glossary.

ARAHATA. An experienced and qualified teacher for ECKANKAR classes.

CHELA. A spiritual student.

ECK. The Life Force, the Holy Spirit, or Audible Life Current which sustains all life.

ECKANKAR. Religion of the Light and Sound of God. Also known as the Ancient Science of SOUL TRAVEL. A truly spiritual religion for the individual in modern times, known as the secret path to God via dreams and SOUL TRAVEL. The teachings provide a framework for anyone to explore their own spiritual experiences. Established by Paul Twitchell, the modern-day founder, in 1965.

ECK MASTERS. Spiritual Masters who can assist and protect people in their spiritual studies and travels. The ECK Masters are from a long line of God-Realized SOULS who know the responsibility that goes with spiritual freedom.

HU. The most ancient, secret name for God. The singing of the word HU, pronounced like the word *hue*, is considered a love song to God. It is sung in the ECK Worship Service.

INITIATION. Earned by the ECK member through spiritual unfoldment and service to God. The initiation is a private ceremony in which the individual is linked to the Sound and Light of God.

LIVING ECK MASTER. The title of the spiritual leader of ECKANKAR. His duty is to lead SOULS back to God. The Living ECK Master can assist spiritual students physically as the Outer Master, in the dream state as the Dream Master, and in the spiritual worlds as the Inner Master. Sri Harold Klemp became the Living ECK Master in 1981.

MAHANTA. A title to describe the highest state of God Consciousness on earth, often embodied in the LIVING ECK MASTER. He is the Living Word.

PLANES. The levels of heaven, such as the Astral, Causal, Mental, Etheric, and Soul planes.

SATSANG. A class in which students of ECK study a monthly lesson from ECKANKAR.

THE SHARIYAT-KI-SUGMAD. The sacred scriptures of ECKANKAR. The scriptures are comprised of twelve volumes in the spiritual worlds. The first two were transcribed from the inner PLANES by Paul Twitchell, modern-day founder of ECKANKAR.

SOUL. The True Self. The inner, most sacred part of each person. Soul exists before birth and lives on after the death of the physical body. As a spark of God, Soul can see, know, and perceive all things. It is the creative center of Its own world.

SOUL TRAVEL. The expansion of consciousness. The ability of SOUL to transcend the physical body and travel into the spiritual worlds of God. Soul Travel is taught only by the LIVING ECK MASTER. It helps people unfold spiritually and can provide proof of the existence of God and life after death.

SOUND AND LIGHT OF ECK. The Holy Spirit. The two aspects through which God appears in the lower worlds. People can experience them by looking and listening within themselves and through SOUL TRAVEL.

SPIRITUAL EXERCISES OF ECK. The daily practice of certain techniques to get us in touch with the Light and Sound of God.

SUGMAD. A sacred name for God. SUGMAD is neither masculine nor feminine; IT is the source of all life.

WAH Z. The spiritual name of Sri Harold Klemp. It means the Secret Doctrine. It is his name in the spiritual worlds.

Index

Index

Being
  Divine, 129. *See also* God
  exact, 374
  positive, 339
  spiritual, 257. *See also* Soul
Belief(s), 290, 300
Bells, 295–96
Bible, 154
Bicycle, 55–57, 225–27
Bird(s). *See also* Blackbirds;
    Blue jays; Cardinals;
    Crows; Dove(s); Duck(s);
    Eagles; Geese; Parrot;
    Redwing blackbirds;
    Robins; Sparrow(s)
  feeding, 161–62, 253–54,
    323–24
  need love, 111
  and Soul, 103, 123
  sound of, 292
Bird feeder, 161–62, 323–24
Birdseed, 211
Blackbirds, 323
Blame, 171
Blasphemy, 287
Blessings, 185, 259, 261, 276
Blue jays, 162
Blue Star
  of ECK, 294, 299
  of the Mahanta, 117
Body
  and heaven, 368, 385
  as house for Soul, 123, 279
  human, 30, 123
  out of the, 10, 25–26, 36, 350
  physical, 25, 27, 36, 42
  Soul, 183
Book, 117–18. *See also*
    ECKANKAR: book(s)
Bookcase, 217–18
Bravery, 161, 200
Buck, 69–70
Bus, 49–50, 83–84
Business, 97, 204
Busy signal, 205

Cadillac, 165
Calamity Jane, 377
Calm, 29, 116, 165, 166
Camels, 33
Campbell, Joseph, 119
Cancer, 327
Candle, 286
Car
  brake, 61–62
  Holy Spirit communicates
    through, 269–71
  lost, 333–35
  -repair show, 269–70
  stalled, 157–59
  visualizing a, 223–24
Cardinals, 323
Care (caring), 3, 255, 374
Caruthers, Mr., 119–20
Cat(s), 163, 377
Catholic man, 113–14
Causal Plane. *See* Plane(s):
    Causal
Cause and effect, 63, 296, 299,
    352
Change
  adjusting to, 214, 235
  through giving, 76, 104
  through the Holy Spirit,
    338
  open to, 328–29
  others, 116, 123, 131–32
  and Spiritual Exercises of
    ECK. *See* Spiritual
    Exercise(s) of ECK:
    changing through
Chanhassen, Minnesota, 249
Channel, 223, 328
Charity, 101, 150, 154, 165–67
Chatter, 349
Checkers, 351–52
Chela, 4, 19–21, 241
Chicken sandwich, 365–66
Child(ren)
  and HU, 109, 117–18, 125
  -like attitude, 363

Index

ECKist(s). *See also* Initiate
  becoming an, 275
  and compassion, 139
  helping others, 349–50
  and history of
    ECKANKAR, 331
  and the Law of Noninter-
    ference, 172
  learn from non-ECKists,
    339–40
  learn to hear the Holy
    Spirit, 171, 229
  life for, 36
  meeting loved ones on the
    inner planes, 183–84
  receiving protection, 177–
    79, 193–94
  responsibility of, 172
  and service, 80
  serving the Mahanta, 321
  and society, 289–90
  and spiritual light, 92, 283,
    343
  and the Temple of ECK,
    131
ECK Master(s). *See also*
    Dream Master; Gopal
    Das; Inner Master; Living
    ECK Master; Mahanta;
    Master; Peddar Zaskq;
    Rebazar Tarzs; Twitchell,
    Paul; Wah Z; Yaubl
    Sacabi
  experience with, 359–60
  help from, 33–34, 265
  on the inner planes, 9–11,
    34, 155, 331–32
  meeting, 9–11, 33–34
  at the Temple of ECK, 353
ECK Worship Service, 305–6
Ecstasy, 209
Education, 42
Effects. *See* Cause and effect
Effort, 206, 224
Electrical wire, 191

Emotion, 80, 83, 104, 154. *See
    also* Plane(s): Astral
Energy (energies), 19, 21, 91–
    93, 165
Enlightenment, 144, 306–7, 343
Etheric Plane. *See* Plane(s):
    Etheric
Euphoria, 209
Excellence, 373–74, 386
Expectations, 382
Experience(s)
  and belief, 290, 300
  benefit from others, 204, 335
  inner, 16–17, 42, 55, 241,
    267, 268, 286
  learning by, 290, 300, 335
  of leaving the old con-
    sciousness, 214
  recognizing spiritual, 366
  of Soul, 103, 123, 370, 376
  tap into past, 370
  understanding, 156
Experiment, 273
Expert, 373–74, 386
Explorers, 164
Expression, 103
Eyes, 9, 82, 96, 116, 275, 294,
    359. *See* Spiritual Eye

Facing
  problem, 257
  yourself, 171
Failure, 204, 257
Faith, 170
Family. *See also* Child(ren)
  of animals. *See* Animals
  being a Co-worker with
    God in, 140
  decisions, 95, 145–46
  of life, 167
  and love, 40
  problems, 33–34, 83, 170, 275
  and spiritual exercises, 109,
    117
Faults, 153–54, 171

Jade master, 381–83, 386
Jehovah's Witness, 337–38
Jesus, 285
Job(s), 213, 293. *See also*
    Making a living; Profes-
    sion; Work
Joke, 47
Journal, 23–24. *See also*
    Dream(s): journal
Journey, 215–16, 376
Joy, 59, 297, 363, 373

Kal, 380
Karma (karmic). *See also*
    Law(s): of Karma
    on the Causal Plane, 296
    fear of, 139
    and idle thoughts, 36
    not taking on others', 139,
        150
    problems, 13, 221
    working out, 36, 257, 385
Key(s), 363, 379–80
Kittens, 163
Knowledge, 14, 208, 366

Language, 125
Laughter, 72–73, 132, 157
Law(s)
    of God, 54, 64
    of Karma, 352
    of Noninterference, 149–50,
        172
    spiritual, 307
    student, 145–46
Learn(ing), 382–83. *See also*
    Lessons
    to be aware, 195
    in a community, 161–62
    in each lifetime, 215, 369–
        70
    by experience, 156, 235, 335
    by hardship, 171
    of the heart. *See* Heart:
        learning of the

about the HU, 188
on the inner planes, 368
to listen, 171
from nature, 211
from others, 335
Leaving, 214, 235
Lesson(s)
    about daily chores, 141
    in ECK, 36
    about love, 254
    for moving to the next
        level, 120
    from previous incarnations,
        369–70
    from silver dollar, 354
    spiritual, 158, 169, 204, 235,
        365
    about spiritual freedom,
        227
    teacher's, 151–52
    about tolerance, 139
    by watching others, 204
Letter, 253
Level, 120
License plate, 153–54
Life
    appreciation for, 297
    better, 247, 377
    change our, 214, 235
    and consciousness, 88
    cutting edge of, 223
    daily, 3–4, 97, 142, 229
    difficulties of, 214, 247, 253,
        257, 375
    direction to take in, 145–
        46, 381
    easier, 259
    of ECK, 36, 350
    force, 291
    game of, 370
    gives to us, 254, 261
    and growth, 319
    help through, 50–51, 229
    inner, 300
    inner and outer, 41

Index

Index

How to Learn More about ECKANKAR
Religion of the Light and Sound of God

Why are you as important to God as any famous head of state, priest, minister, or saint that ever lived?

- Do you know God's purpose in your life?
- Why does God's Will seem so unpredictable?
- Why do you talk to God, but practice no one religion?

ECKANKAR can show you why special attention from God is neither random nor reserved for the few known saints. But it is for every individual. It is for anyone who opens himself to Divine Spirit, the Light and Sound of God.

People want to know the secrets of life and death. In response to this need Sri Harold Klemp, today's spiritual leader of ECKANKAR, and Paul Twitchell, its modern-day founder, have written a series of monthly discourses that give specialized Spiritual Exercises of ECK. They can lead Soul in a direct way to God.

Those who wish to study ECKANKAR can receive these special monthly discourses which give clear, simple instructions for these spiritual exercises.

Membership in ECKANKAR Includes

1. The opportunity to gain wisdom, charity, and spiritual freedom.
2. Twelve monthly discourses which include information on Soul, the spiritual meaning of dreams, Soul Travel techniques, and ways to establish a personal relationship with Divine Spirit. You may study them alone at home or in a class with others.
3. The *Mystic World*, a quarterly newsletter with a Wisdom Note and articles by the Living ECK Master. In it are also letters and articles from members of ECKANKAR around the world.
4. Special mailings to keep you informed of upcoming ECKANKAR seminars and activities worldwide, new study materials available from ECKANKAR, and more.
5. The opportunity to attend ECK Satsang classes and book discussions with others in your community.
6. Initiation eligibility.
7. Attendance at certain meetings for members of ECKANKAR at ECK seminars.

How to Find Out More

To request membership in ECKANKAR using your credit card (or for a free booklet on membership) call (612) 544-0066, weekdays, between 8:00 a.m. and 5:00 p.m., central time. Or write to: ECKANKAR, Att: Information, P.O. Box 27300, Minneapolis, MN 55427 U.S.A.

Introductory Books on ECKANKAR

Ask the Master, Book 1
Harold Klemp

"What is my purpose in life?" "Are dreams real?" "How do past lives affect us today?" Harold Klemp, as the spiritual leader of ECKANKAR, gives clear and candid answers to these and other questions which people have asked throughout history and ask today in letters he receives from around the globe. His answers can help you overcome fear, learn self-discipline, be more creative, and improve family relationships.

ECKANKAR—Ancient Wisdom for Today

Are you one of the millions who have heard God speak to you through a profound spiritual experience? This introductory book will show you how dreams, Soul Travel, and experiences with past lives are ways God speaks to you. An entertaining, easy-to-read approach to ECKANKAR. Reading this little book can give you new perspectives on your spiritual life.

The Spiritual Exercises of ECK
Harold Klemp

This book is a staircase with 131 steps. It's a special staircase, because you don't have to climb all the steps to get to the top. Each step is a spiritual exercise, a way to help you explore your inner worlds. And what awaits you at the top? The doorway to spiritual freedom, self-mastery, wisdom, and love.

Dreams, A Source of Inner Truth
(Audiocassette)

Dreams are windows into worlds beyond the ordinary. This two-tape set can help you open these windows through insights and spiritual exercises given by Sri Harold Klemp, spiritual leader of ECKANKAR.

For fastest service, phone (612) 544-0066 weekdays between 8:00 a.m. and 5:00 p.m., central time, to request books using your credit card, or look under **ECKANKAR** in your phone book for an ECKANKAR Center near you. Or write:**ECKANKAR, Att: Information, P.O. Box 27300, Minneapolis, MN 55427 U.S.A.**

There May Be an
ECKANKAR Study Group near You

ECKANKAR offers a variety of local and international activities for the spiritual seeker. With hundreds of study groups worldwide, ECKANKAR is near you! Many areas have ECKANKAR Centers where you can browse through the books in a quiet, unpressured environment, talk with others who share an interest in this ancient teaching, and attend beginning discussion classes on how to gain the attributes of Soul: wisdom, power, love, and freedom.

Around the world, ECKANKAR study groups offer special one-day or weekend seminars on the basic teachings of ECKANKAR. Check your phone book under **ECKANKAR**, ☎ or call **(612) 544-0066** for membership information and the location of the ECKANKAR Center or study group nearest you. Or write **ECKANKAR, Att: Information, P.O. Box 27300, Minneapolis, MN 55427 U.S.A.**

☐ Please send me information on the nearest ECKANKAR discussion or study group in my area.

☐ Please send me more information about membership in ECKANKAR, which includes a twelve-month spiritual study.

Please type or print clearly   940

Name _____

Street_____ Apt. # _____

City _____ State/Prov. _____

ZIP/Postal Code _____ Country _____